LOTUS NOTES®
FOR NOVICES

LOTUS NOTES®
FOR NOVICES

A GUIDE FOR THE PERPLEXED

WINDOWS® EDITION

ALLEN W. SIM

BALLANTINE BOOKS • NEW YORK

Copyright ©1994 by Random House, Inc.

All rights reserved under International and Pan-American Copyright Conventions. Published in the United States by Ballantine Books, a division of Random House, Inc., New York and simultaneously in Canada by Random House of Canada, Limited, Toronto, Canada.

Lotus and Lotus Notes are registered trademarks of the Lotus Development Corporation.

Windows is a trademark of Microsoft Corporation.

The author and publisher have used their best efforts in preparing this book and the data contained herein. However, the author and publisher make no warranties of any kind, express or implied, with regard to the documentation, program listings, techniques, or data contained in this book. Neither the author nor publisher shall be responsible or liable for any loss of profit or any commercial damages, including but not limited to special, incidental, consquential, or any other damages in connection with, or arising out of, use of this book.

Library of Congress Catalog Card Number: 94-94632

ISBN 0-345-39385-6

Cover designed by Richard Hasselberger

Manufactured in the United States of America

First Edition: September 1994

10 9 8 7 6 5 4 3 2 1

Contents

1. Getting Started 1

    About This Book.. 1

    What Is Lotus Notes?.. 2

    How Will Notes Help Me? 3

    How Does Notes Work?... 3

    Starting Notes 5

    Logging On to a Network 5

    Exiting Notes 6

2. The Main Window 7

    Title Bar... 8

    Menu Bar.. 9

    SmartIcons (Tool Bar).. 10

    Workspace Window 11

    Status Bar.. 13

3. Working with Databases 17

    Opening a Database 17

    Opening a Database from Its Icon 22

    Database Windows 23

    Closing a Database... 25

    Managing Database Icons 25

    Creating a New Database.................................. 29

    Deleting a Database.. 33

    Access Control Lists... 34

4. Database Views..35

Categories and Documents 36

Selecting a View... 38

View SmartIcons 38

Getting Around 38

Expanding and Contracting the View............................... 40

Refreshing the View 42

5. Reading Documents 43

Opening a Document 43

Getting Around 44

Special Features 44

Attachments 45

Buttons 47

Doclinks... 47

Pop-Ups 48

Searching for Text... 49

Paging Through the Database 51

Printing the Active Document.. 51

Closing the Active Document 53

6. Editing Documents 55

Documents and Fields 55

Edit Document SmartIcons 56

Creating a New Document... 56

Putting a Document in Edit Mode 59

Basic Editing Commands 60

Headers and Footers 63

Checking Your Spelling... 64

Saving Your Changes 65

7. Editing Rich Text 67

Attachments 67

Buttons 70

Doclinks.. 70

Importing a File 72

OLE Objects 74

Pop-Ups 79

Resizing a Picture 81

Special Characters.. 82

Creating and Editing Tables... 89

Formatting Tables.. 94

8. Formatting Rich Text...99

Applying Fonts 99

Formatting Paragraphs 105

Paragraph Styles... 112

9. Managing Documents 119

Selecting Documents 119

Marking Documents Read or Unread 122

Categorizing Documents.. 124

Moving and Copying Documents 126

Deleting Documents... 126

Printing Views and Documents 128

10. Searching a Database 133

Performing a Plain Text Search 133

Full Text Indices 135

Performing a Full Text Search 140

11. Notes Mail 147

Notes Mail and Databases... 147

Mail SmartIcons 147

Using Mail Over a Modem.. 148

Opening Your Mail 149

Writing Mail 150

Address Books 152

Forwarding Documents 153

12. Notes Remote: Using a Modem 157

Getting Set Up... 157

Remote SmartIcons 157

Calling a Server.. 158

Hanging Up 159

What Is Replication? 159

Creating a Replica.. 160

Performing Replication.. 161

13. Modifying Your Setup............................165

Changing Your Password 165

Date and Time Settings....................................... 167

Selecting a Printer.. 168

Customizing Your SmartIcons 169

14. Odds and Ends 173

Manipulating Secondary Windows....................... 173

Stopping Notes... 177

Using Notes Help 177

Appendix 1: Common Limits 181

Appendix 2: Glossary 183

Index 191

CHAPTER 1

Getting Started

About This Book

Lotus Notes for Novices is primarily intended for the inexperienced Lotus Notes®
user who wants to get up and running fast. It is not intended as a comprehensive
guide, but as a fast, accessible resource for the user who is new to Notes, has real
work to do, and needs to get moving.

The above caveat aside, *Lotus Notes for Novices* contains tips that users of all
levels will find helpful, and discussions of Notes' nuances that even an experienced user will find illuminating.

Operating Systems

Notes is available for Microsoft Windows®, OS/2®, and the Apple Macintosh®.
This book covers Lotus Notes for Windows. Since the Windows and OS/2
versions of Notes are almost identical, users should find this book helpful with
the OS/2 version as well. In the interest of simplicity, we have not included
specific directions for OS/2.

Since *Lotus Notes for Novices* is intended for beginners, it also covers some of the
basics of using Windows. If you are *not* new to Windows, but *are* new to Notes,
you can skip over the sections that explain standard Windows features and
functionality. The author and editors have attempted to flag the major sections
that can be ignored by the more experienced Windows user.

Keyboard Instructions

Many Windows features and functions can be accessed from the keyboard using
a combination of keys. These combinations are referred to as *hot keys*, *accelerator
keys*, or *short-cut keys*. In this book, a key's title is surrounded in angle brackets

("<>"), and a plus sign ("+") is used to connect keys that should be pressed simultaneously. For example, "press <Alt> + <X>" means "hold <Alt> down while you press <X>".

Defined Terms

New terms are defined as they are introduced, and also appear in the Glossary (see page 183).

Using This Book

In general, *Lotus Notes for Novices* is meant to be read from front to back, but you should feel free to skip the stuff you don't care about, and to jump to topics that interest and concern you. Once you're up and running, the book serves as a good "how to" reference.

The first two chapters — the current one and "The Main Window" on page 7 — cover what Notes does and what it looks like. The rest of the book covers more specific subjects, such as working with databases or using Notes mail.

How This Book Was Created

Lotus Notes for Novices was written in Microsoft Word for Windows® 2.0c. The graphics were created using Tiffany Plus® 1.51U, Paint Shop Pro® 2.01, CorelDRAW!® 3.00B, and Paintbrush®. The author's computer is a Gateway 2000® 486DX/33 with a Gateway CrystalScan® 1776 LE monitor and a Gateway fax/modem. He uses MS-DOS 6.2® and Windows for Workgroups 3.11®.

The author and editors communicated and coordinated using Lotus Notes. The book's source files were sent to the publisher in compressed form attached to a Notes Mail document. The author connected to the publisher's network via modem.

What Is Lotus Notes?

Lotus Notes is the premier entry in an emerging field of software known as *groupware*. Groupware allows groups of users to work together by sharing information across a computer network. The information can include files created in Notes, files from other software packages, comments attached to those files, and a variety of other file formats and types of information. You can also combine different types of information and different file formats into a single Notes document or database. The possibilities are essentially endless.

How Will Notes Help Me?

The following are some of the benefits that current users have reported:

- Simplifies and improves coordination of projects
- Integrates personnel from different locations
- Reduces and speeds busywork, freeing time for real, productive work
- Cuts development time by shortening bureaucratic lag. Team members have constant, ready access to the current project information.
- Encourages and channels ideas and suggestions from all team members, regardless of areas of expertise or responsibility. One user dubbed this phenomenon "intellectual cross-pollination."

How Does Notes Work?

Notes has been described as a free-form database program, a description that strikes many computer users as an oxymoron. That reaction is valid, but so is the description — Notes has more in common with database programs than with any other type of application, even though its approach to data is very different. Like a database program, Notes is a tool for grouping and controlling information. Unlike database programs, the information can be widely divergent in form and format.

What Is a Conventional Database?

A conventional database is related information that is stored according to a predetermined format. The format is based on the data's significant characteristics. For example, a telephone book is a database in printed form. The significant characteristics are name, address, and telephone number. Most people think of a conventional database as a table, with each row containing a data entry and each column containing a data characteristic.

What Does a Database Program Do?

A database program creates and manipulates databases that are stored on a computer. One of the simplest and most common uses for a database program is to create and maintain a mailing list that contains the same information as the telephone book that was mentioned above.

How Is Notes Different?

In Notes, information resides in *documents*, and documents reside in *databases*. A Notes document can contain many different types of data, and a Notes database can provide a variety of ways to organize its documents. The conventional database metaphor of a table with orderly rows and columns does not apply to Notes.

Notes Documents

True to the name, the typical Notes document is all or mostly text, but a document can also contain graphics, embedded files from other software packages, even multimedia elements. Documents can be linked to other documents, providing easy access to related information. A document can also have attached "child" documents that can contain other team member's comments on the original "parent" document.

Notes Databases

A Notes database is a collection of documents, all of which share certain pre-defined characteristics. These characteristics can be minimal or complex. For example, a database could consist of documents with four characteristics: the document's title, the author's name, the date and time the document was created, and the document's text.

Notes E-Mail

Notes also comes with its own electronic mail, another feature that separates it from conventional database programs. Notes Mail is a complete e-mail system. For help using Notes Mail, see page 147.

How Do You Use Notes?

Using Notes is a tough act to describe. Everything you do in Notes starts with opening a database, but from there the paths are endless. You might edit one of the database's documents, or you might create a new one. You might view a document that someone else created and send them comments. Or the database you opened might be designed for on-line discussions, much like a forum on Compuserve® or Prodigy®.

Again, Notes is like a database program in that it is a tool for grouping and controlling information, but unlike a database program in that the information can be widely divergent in form and format. And since the data can be richly varied, so are the things that you may find yourself doing with Lotus Notes.

Starting Notes

Like most Windows applications, you start Notes by double-clicking[1] on its icon[2]. Where the Notes icon is located depends on how your system is configured. For most users, the icon is in the Lotus Notes group in the Program Manager. If you can't find the Notes icon, ask your technical support person or a knowledgeable friend or associate for help.

When you start Notes, its system logo will appear briefly, followed by the Notes main window. See "The Main Window" on page 7.

Logging On to a Network

When you start Notes, the system will probably present the Enter Password Dialog Box (see diagram on the following page). Type your password into the main text box. If you want Notes to automatically log-off if you're not using it, press <Tab> to access the small text box at the bottom of the dialog box, then type the number of minutes that you want Notes to remain idle before logging off. If you don't care about automatically logging off, leave the text box empty. When you have entered your password and set the idle time, press <Enter>.

---

[1] **Clicking & Double-Clicking:** You click on something by using the mouse to place the cursor over the item and pressing the *primary mouse button* once. For most users, the primary mouse button is the one on the left. If you're left-handed, it may be on the right. Double-clicking is just like clicking only you press the primary mouse button twice in rapid succession. If you can't get the hang of double-clicking, your mouse's double-click speed may be set too fast. Ask your technical support person or a knowledgeable friend or coworker for help.

[2] **Icon:** An icon is a small picture that represents a program, a function, a data file, or anything that a programmer wants it to. The most common use of icons is to represent programs that can be launched from the Windows Shell. For most users, the Windows Shell is Program Manager.

Enter Password Dialog Box

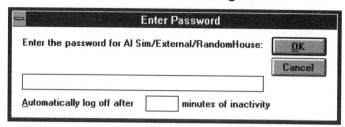

Exiting Notes

You exit Notes like most Windows programs. You can:

▶ Select "Exit" from the File menu,

▶ Press <Alt> + <F4>, or

▶ Double-click on the main window's Control box.

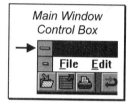

CHAPTER 2

The Main Window

When you start Notes, you'll probably see something like the diagram below, which shows a typical example of the Notes *main window*. The main window encompasses and controls the important functional areas that you use to do your work. This chapter explains each of these functional areas as they appear in the example shown here, starting at the top with the title bar and working down to the Status Bar.

Notes Main Window (Example)

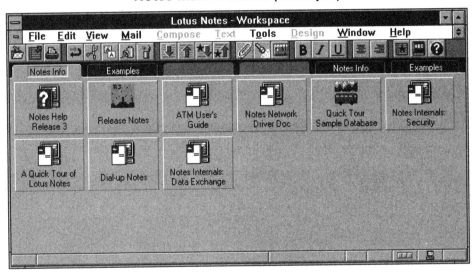

Important! Notes' documentation calls the main window the *Workspace*, even though the main window contains a secondary window[1] with the same name (see "Workspace Window" on page 11). In this book, "Workspace" or "Workspace Window" always refers to the secondary window.

---

[1] **Secondary Window:** In general, a secondary window is where you get your hands on the data. In Notes, the secondary windows are where you work with databases and documents.

> **Please Note:** If you are new to Windows, this chapter provides an introduction to some standard Windows features. If you are *not* new to Windows, but *are* new to Notes, you can skim this chapter. Sections of particular interest are marked with a "☑".

Title Bar

Lotus Notes - Workspace

The Notes title bar is a standard Windows title bar. As the name implies, it displays the program's title. If one of the program's secondary windows is active[2] and maximized[3], its name follows the program's name, separated by a dash. In the example above, the Workspace secondary window is active and maximized, hence "Lotus Notes - Workspace".

> **Tip:** Double-clicking on the text display section of the title bar switches the window between its maximized and normal states.

The rest of the Notes title bar contains the standard title bar controls.

Control Box and the Control Menu

Control Box

At the left end of the title bar is the Control box, which you use to access the Main Window Control menu (see diagram below). Double-clicking on the Control box closes Notes.

To open the Control menu, click on the Control box, or press <Alt> + <Spacebar>. You can use the Control menu to position the main window, to exit Notes, or to access your system's task manager. You choose a menu selection by clicking on it, pressing its underlined letter, or using the cursor keys to highlight it and pressing <Enter>.

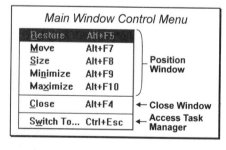

---

[2] **Active Window:** The active window is the one that is currently receiving keyboard input.

[3] **Maximized:** A window is maximized when it occupies all of its available space.

Positioning Buttons

At the right end of the title bar are the window's positioning buttons. In the example shown above, the Minimize and Maximize buttons are present. When the window is maximized, the Maximize button is replaced by the Restore button.

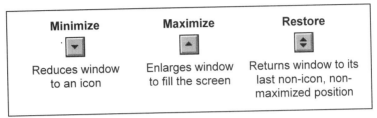

Menu Bar

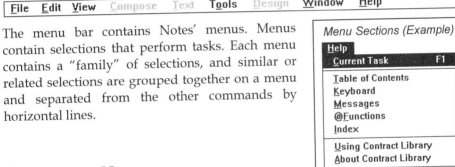

The menu bar contains Notes' menus. Menus contain selections that perform tasks. Each menu contains a "family" of selections, and similar or related selections are grouped together on a menu and separated from the other commands by horizontal lines.

Opening a Menu

You open a menu by clicking on it, or by pressing <Alt> plus the letter that is underlined in the menu's title. For example, to open the Help menu, you would press <Alt> + <H>.

Choosing a Menu Selection

You choose a menu selection by clicking on it, pressing its underlined letter, or using the cursor keys to highlight it and pressing <Enter>. To find out what a selection does, see "What Does This Menu Selection Do?" on the following page.

☑ *What Does This Menu Selection Do?*

When you highlight a menu selection, Notes uses the title bar to display a brief description of the selection. To see a selection's description, open the menu (see the preceding page) and use the cursor keys to highlight the selection.

Menu Help (Example)

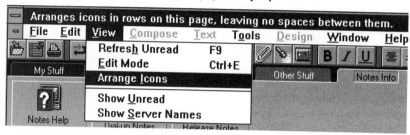

SmartIcons (Tool Bar)

Just below the menu bar is a row of buttons, which Lotus calls "SmartIcons". In most Windows programs, these are called tool bar buttons, and the whole row is referred to as the tool bar.

Using a SmartIcon

SmartIcons perform an action, just like a menu selection. Using a SmartIcon couldn't be easier — just click on it. To find out what a SmartIcon does, see "What Does This SmartIcon Do?" below.

☑ *What Does This SmartIcon Do?*

To find out what a SmartIcon does, point at it and press and hold the secondary mouse button[4]. Notes will use the title bar to display a brief explanation of the SmartIcon's action (see diagram on the following page). To get more information, look for the corresponding menu selection. For example, to get

---

[4] **Secondary Mouse Button:** On a two-button mouse, the secondary button is the one that you use less often. For most users, it's the right button. If you're left-handed, your buttons may be reversed, in which case the secondary button would be on the left.

more help with the SmartIcon shown below, highlight the "Paste" selection on the Edit menu ("Edit Paste"). See "What Does This Menu Selection Do?" on the preceding page.

SmartIcon Help (Example)

☑ *Can I Change My SmartIcons?*

You can select a different set of SmartIcons by using the SmartIcons button (see page 15) on the Status Bar (see page 13). For help creating and editing sets of SmartIcons, see "Customizing Your SmartIcons" on page 169.

☑ Workspace Window

The Workspace is a secondary window[5] that holds database icons. It contains six of what Lotus calls "tabbed pages", which look something like file folders. You use the tabbed pages to group database icons. You cannot add or delete pages, and you cannot rearrange the page order.

> **Important!** The documentation that comes with Notes also refers to the main window (see page 7) as the *Workspace*. In this book, "Workspace" or "Workspace Window" always refers to the window defined above.

---

5 For help with secondary windows, see "Manipulating Secondary Windows" on page 173.

Accessing the Workspace

If the Workspace window isn't visible, you can select it from the bottom section of the Windows menu.

🖱 Click on "Window" in the menu bar, then click on "Workspace".

⌨ Press <Alt> + <W>, then <1>.

☑ Selecting a Page

The easiest way to select a page is to click on its tab. The tab of the active page is always light gray, the same color as the page itself, and the text is recessed.

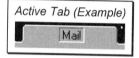

Active Tab (Example)

Mail

⌨ You use the cursor keys to select a page with the keyboard. Press <Ctrl> + < ←> to move to the previous page. Press <Ctrl> + <→> to move to the next page. When a tab is active, you do not have to press <Ctrl> to use the arrow keys, and you can move to the first tab by pressing <Home> and the last by pressing <End>.

☑ Database Icons

As the name implies, a database icon represents a database. For more help with database icons, see "Opening a Database from Its Icon" on page 22 and "Managing Database Icons" on page 25. For help with databases in general, see "Working with Databases" on page 17.

Database Icon
(Example)

Requisition
Approvals

☑ Editing the Tabs

Notes Info   My Stuff   Examples

To set a tab's color or title:

🖱 Double-click on it.

⌨ Use the cursor keys to highlight it, then press <Enter>. A tab is highlighted when its text appears indented.

Notes will open the Workspace Page
Name dialog box.

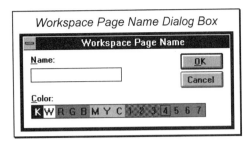

Workspace Page Name Dialog Box

▶ To change the tab's settings,
follow the directions below,
then click on the OK button
or press <Alt> + <O>.

▶ To close the dialog box
without changing the tab's
settings, click on the Cancel button or press <Esc>.

Title

You enter the title into the Name text box. To put the cursor in the text box, click
in it, or press <Alt> + <N>.

Color

To select a color, click on it in the row of colored squares (which appear as
shades of gray in the diagram above). To select a color with the keyboard, press
<Alt> + <C>, then use the cursor keys to highlight the square, or press the
color's underlined character. For example, to select blue, press <Alt> + <C>, then
press <B>.

☑ Status Bar

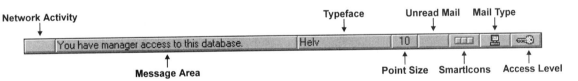

Network Activity

Typeface

Unread Mail   Mail Type

You have manager access to this database.   Helv   10

Message Area

Point Size   SmartIcons   Access Level

The Status Bar appears at the bottom of the Main Window. It is divided into
eight unequal segments, each of which has a specific function. Most of the
segments display text or pictures that provide information about Notes' current
state (hence "Status Bar"), and some segments access functions.

Please Note: The rest of this section covers the Status Bar in detail and is intended
for reference, not as an introduction. If you are new to Notes, you may
prefer to skip ahead to the next chapter. See "Working with Databases"
on page 17.

Network Activity Indicator

The Network Activity Indicator displays a lightning bolt during network activity. Examples of network activity include opening a shared database and sending or receiving mail.

Network
Activity

 ## Message Area

The Message Area displays various messages about your current activities. Clicking on the Message Area opens a pop-up that lists the nine most recent messages. Click on the pop-up to close it.

Message Area Pop-Up Display (Example)

Looking for HELP
No matching documents were found.
25 documents found
Some highlights are not visible with this form
No matching documents were found.
More than 250 matching documents were found.
135 documents found
Some highlights are not visible with this form
11 documents found

Typeface Indicator

The Typeface Indicator displays the typeface at the insertion point[6]. The indicator is active when you're in Edit Mode, and blank when you're not. It is also blank when the insertion point spans paragraphs with different fonts. Clicking on the indicator opens a typeface pop-up menu. To choose a typeface:

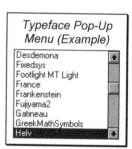

Typeface Pop-Up Menu (Example)

Desdemona
Fixedsys
Footlight MT Light
France
Frankenstein
Fujiyama2
Gatineau
GreekMathSymbols
Helv

  Click on it.

  Use the cursor keys to highlight it and press <Enter>. You can move through the list by pressing character keys. For example, pressing <F> will take you to the first typeface that begins with "F", and pressing <F> again will take you to the second typeface that begins with "F".

---

[6] **Insertion Point:** The insertion point is where Notes will insert new text. It is either the cursor or the currently highlighted text. Notes will delete highlighted text when you start typing.

☑ *Point Size Indicator*

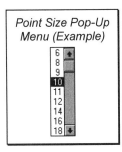

Point Size Pop-Up Menu (Example)

The Point Size Indicator displays the text size at the insertion point. The indicator is active when you're in Edit Mode, and blank when you're not. It is also blank when the insertion point spans paragraphs with different fonts. Clicking on the indicator opens a point size pop-up menu. To choose a point size:

 Click on it.

 Use the cursor keys to highlight it and press <Enter>. You can move through the list by pressing number keys. For example, pressing <2> will take you to the first point size that begins with "2", and pressing <2> again will take you to the second point size that begins with "2".

☑ *Mail Indicator*

Mail Indicator

The Mail Indicator displays an envelope (see diagram at right) if you have unread mail, and is blank if you do not. Clicking on the envelope accesses your mail, and displays the last view that you used. For help with Notes Mail, see page 147.

☑ *SmartIcons Button*

SmartIcons Button

Clicking on the SmartIcons button opens a pop-up menu that controls the SmartIcons. To choose a set of SmartIcons:

 Click on it.

 Use the cursor keys to highlight it and press <Enter>. You can move through the list by pressing letter keys. For example, pressing <D> will take you to the first selection that begins with "D", and pressing <D> again will move to the second selection that begins with "D".

SmartIcons Pop-Up Menu

Default Set
Design
Edit Document
Mail
Remote
View Navigation
Working Together
Hide SmartIcons

☑ *Mail Type Indicator*

Display	Meaning
🖧	You're using network-based mail
🖥	You're using workstation-based mail or non-Notes mail

The Mail Type Indicator shows whether Notes is set up for network-based mail, or for workstation-based mail or non-Notes mail, such as cc:Mail®. (For help with Notes Mail, see page 147.) For more information about your mail setup, click on the Mail Type Indicator. Notes will display a more complete description in the Message Area.

Mail Message (Example)

You are set up to use None.

☑ *Access Level Indicator*

🔑 Manager		📝 Editor		👓 Reader	
⚙ Designer		✒ Author		📥 Depositor	

The Access Level Indicator displays your access level for the active database. For help with access levels, see "Access Control Lists" on page 34. For more information about your current access level, click on the Access Level Indicator. Notes will display a description in the Message Area.

Access Level Message (Example)

You have manager access to this database.

CHAPTER 3

Working with Databases

A Notes database is a collection of documents that share certain pre-defined characteristics. These characteristics can be simple or complex.

> **Important!** Every database has an *Access Control List*. The list specifies which users can open the database and what tasks they can perform. If you cannot open a database, or perform some task within the database (such as opening a particular document), it is probably because of your standing in the Access Control List. For more help, see "Access Control Lists" on page 34.

Opening a Database

When you open a database, Notes automatically places its icon on the current Workspace page. This section explains how you open a database that does not yet have an icon in your Workspace. For help opening a database from its icon, see page 22.

To open a database, you need to know which *server* it's on. A server is a computer that houses databases. A server can be your own PC, or a computer on your network that serves as a database library. If someone you know uses the database, they can tell you which server it's on (see "Getting a Database's Server" on page 21). If not, ask your technical support person or a knowledgeable coworker for help.

To open a database, follow these steps:

1 Select the Workspace Window

If the Workspace is not visible, select it from the bottom section of the Windows menu.

Click on "Window" in the menu bar, then click on "Workspace".

Press <Alt> + <W>, then <1>.

Click on the Workspace SmartIcon.

2 Select the Page for the Icon

Notes puts the icon for the new database on the current page. The easiest way to select a page is to click on its tab. The tab of the active page is always light gray, the same color as the page itself. For help selecting a page with the keyboard, see "Selecting a Page" on page 12.

3 Access the "Open Database" Dialog Box

Click on "File" in the menu bar, then click on "Open Database".

Press <Alt> + <F>, then <O>.

Click on the File Open Database SmartIcon.

Open Database Dialog Box (Example)

4 | Select the Server

You select a server from the Server combo box[1]. To open a database that's on your PC, select "Local". To select a server:

 Double-click on it.

 Use the cursor keys to highlight the server and press <Enter>.

Notes will fill the Database list box with the databases and database subdirectories on the selected server.

Database List Box with Server Selected (Example)

```
ATM User's Guide
Ballantine Notes Users' Forum
Notes Help Release 3
Notes Log [Al Sim/External/Rando
RandomHouse Replica
Release Notes
Sim's Address Book
[DOC]
[EXAMPLES]
[MAIL]
```

5 | Find the Database

If you're lucky, the database you're looking for will appear in the Database list box. If it doesn't, it's probably in one of the server's database subdirectories, which are grouped at the bottom of the list box and appear in all caps within square brackets. In the example above, the entries "[DOC]", "[EXAMPLES]", and "[MAIL]" are database subdirectories. To select a subdirectory:

 Double-click on it.

 Use the cursor keys to highlight it and press <Enter>.

If the database you're looking for isn't in the subdirectory that you open, you can return to the parent directory by selecting the "[...]" entry.

Viewing a Database's Description

To read a description of a particular database, highlight it, then select the About button.

 Click on the database, then click on the About button.

 Use the cursor keys to highlight the database, then press <Alt> + <A>.

---

[1] **Combo Box**: A combo box is a hybrid of a text box and a list box, hence the name. The text section acts upon the list section, allowing you to narrow the list or find an entry by typing text. The text section is the small rectangle at the top of the combo box, and the list section is the larger rectangle at the bottom.

Notes will open the About Database dialog box. You can use the scroll bar[2] or the cursor keys to view the text. To close the About Database dialog box, click on the OK button, or press <Esc>.

About Database Dialog Box (Example)

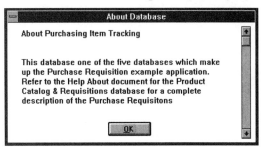

6 Select the Database

🖰 Double-click on the database, or click on it once and click on the Open button.

⌨ Use the cursor keys to highlight the database, then press <Enter> or <Alt> + <O>.

Notes will open the *About Database Document*. The document contains information about the database's purpose. You use the scroll bars or the cursor keys to scroll through the text.

7 Close the "About Database" Document

🖰 Select "Close Window" from the File menu. Click on "File" in the menu bar, then click on "Close Window".

⌨ Press <Ctrl> + <W>.

Notes will close the About Database document and present the database window that displays the current database view.

▶ For help with database windows, see page 23.

▶ For help using views, see "Database Views" on page 35.

▶ For help reading documents, see page 43.

[2] **Scroll Bar:** You use scroll bars to view text or graphics that won't fit in a window, or in some cases, to adjust values. Point at the slider button with the mouse, press the primary mouse button, and drag the slider button in the direction that you want to go. You can also move the slider button by clicking on either side of it, or by clicking on the arrow buttons at either end of the scroll bar.

Slider→
Button

Getting a Database's Server

If someone you know uses a database that you want to use, they can tell you which server it's on. Follow these steps:

1 | Select the Workspace Window

If the Workspace is not visible, select it from the bottom section of the Windows menu.

🖱 Click on "Window" in the menu bar, then click on "Workspace".

⌨ Press <Alt> + <W>, then <1>.

2 | Select the Page that Contains the Database Icon

The easiest way to select a page is to click on its tab. The tab of the active page is always light gray, the same color as the page itself. For help selecting a page with the keyboard, see "Selecting a Page" on page 12.

3 | Highlight the Icon

🖱 Click on it.

⌨ Use the cursor keys. If the tab is highlighted (the text appears indented), press <↓> once to move down onto the page. Pressing <Home> and <End> moves to the first and last icons respectively.

4 | Select "Database" from the "File" Menu

🖱 Click on "File" in the menu bar, then click on "Database".

⌨ Press <Alt> + <F>, then <D>.

Notes will open the Database *sub-menu*. A sub-menu opens out to the right of the parent menu selection. Menu selections that open a sub-menu are followed by a small wedge ("▶").

Database Sub-Menu

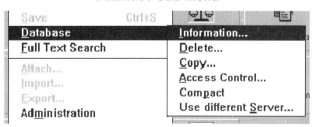

5 Select "Information" from the "Database" Sub-Menu

Click on "Information", or press <I>. Notes will open the Database Information dialog box (see below). If no server is listed in the dialog box, then the database is on your PC.

Database Information Dialog Box

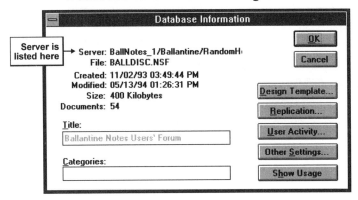

6 Close the "Database Information" Dialog Box

🖱 Click on the Cancel button.

⌨ Press <Esc>.

Opening a Database from Its Icon

To open a database from its icon in the Workspace window, follow these steps:

1 Select the Workspace Window

If the Workspace is not visible, select it from the bottom section of the Windows menu.

🖱 Click on "Window" in the menu bar, then click on "Workspace".

⌨ Press <Alt> + <W>, then <1>.

⊞ Click on the Workspace SmartIcon.

2 Select the Page

The easiest way to select a page is to click on its tab. The tab of the active page is always light gray, the same color as the page itself. For help selecting a page with the keyboard, see "Selecting a Page" on page 12.

3 Select the Icon

You can open a database to the last *view* that you used, or to a specific view. A view is a full or partial list of the database's documents.

Opening the Last-Used View

 Double-click on the icon, or click on it once and press <Enter>.

 If the page's tab is highlighted (the text appears indented), press <↓> once to move down onto the page. Use the cursor keys to highlight the icon, then press <Enter>. Pressing <Home> and <End> moves to the first and last icons respectively.

Opening to a Specific View

You open a database to a specific view by highlighting its icon and selecting a view from the View menu.

 Click once on the icon to highlight it. Click on "View" in the Menu Bar, then click on a view selection.

 If the page's tab is highlighted (the text appears indented), press <↓> once to move down onto the page. Use the cursor keys to highlight the icon. Press <Alt> + <V>, then use the cursor keys to highlight a view selection and press <Enter>.

Database Windows

When you open a database, Notes opens a new *database window*. Database windows are secondary windows[3] that display database *views*. A view is a full or partial list of the database's contents. Views are covered in detail in the next chapter, "Database Views" (see page 35).

Each row in a database window contains either a single document or the heading for a document category. Each column contains one piece of information about the documents. Database windows have unique features that you use to work with the current view.

---

[3] For help with secondary windows, see "Manipulating Secondary Windows" on page 173.

Database Window Features

With Window In Normal State (Non-Maximized, Non-Minimized)

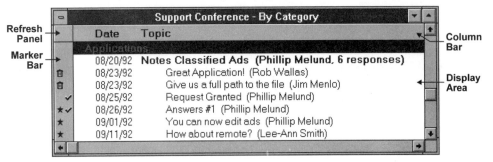

Column Bar

The Column Bar displays the titles of the columns. Each column contains one piece of information about the documents.

Display Area

The Display Area contains the list of categories and documents. You use the scroll bars to scroll through the list. Depending on the database's design, an attachment marker (which looks like a paper clip) may appear next to documents that have files embedded in them.

Attachment Marker ──▶ ⬧ Broadcast Rights Revisted
Pay-Per-View Contracts: Issues, Ideas, etc.
Winetka Advertising Contracts

Marker Bar

The Marker Bar displays symbols that indicate the status of the row's document or category. The following table explains each of the symbols.

Marker Bar Symbols		
Marker	**Name**	**Indicates**
★	*Unread*	Documents you haven't opened or have marked as unread
✔	*Selected*	Selected documents and categories
🗑	*Delete*	Documents marked for deletion
◆	*Conflict*	Duplicate documents. Occurs when document is simultaneously edited by multiple users.

Refresh Panel

Clicking on the Refresh Panel updates the view. In some cases you'll receive a prompt asking if you want to make the changes permanent. A question mark appears if documents are added or deleted while the view is open. For example, if you receive mail while your mail

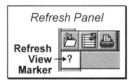

Refresh Panel

Refresh View Marker →

database is open, the Refresh View Marker will appear in the mail database's window.

Closing a Database

Notes lacks a command for closing a database, and it's an annoying omission. The only way to close a database is to close each of the open windows. For help closing a secondary window, see page 177.

Managing Database Icons

You find database icons in the Workspace. For help using the Workspace, see "Workspace Window" on page 11.

Database Icon (Example)

Requisition Approvals

Adding an Icon

Adding a database's icon to the Workspace is similar to opening a database (see page 17). Follow these steps:

1 Select a Workspace Page

Activate the Workspace window and select a page for the database's icon.

2 Access the "Open Database" Dialog Box

Select "Open Database" from the File menu.

🖰 Click on "File" in the menu bar, then click on "Open Database".

⌨ Press <Alt> + <F>, then <O>.

📝 Click on the File Open Database SmartIcon.

The following diagram shows the next four steps. For more help, continue below.

Open Database Dialog Box (Example)

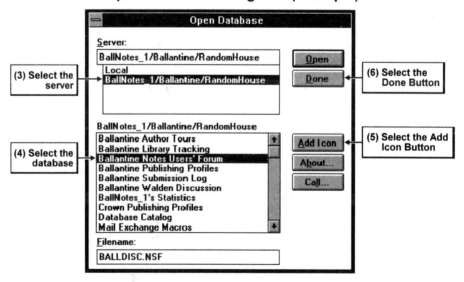

③ Select the Server

You select a server from the Server combo box. To open a database that's on your PC, select "Local".

🖰 Double-click on the server.

⌨ Use the cursor keys to highlight the server and press <Enter>.

④ Select the Database

If you're lucky, the database you're looking for will appear in the Database list box. If it doesn't, it's probably in one of the subdirectories (see below). When you find the database:

🖰 Click on it.

⌨ Use the cursor keys to highlight it.

Selecting a Directory

The subdirectories are grouped at the bottom of the list box and appear in all caps within square brackets. If the database you're looking for isn't in the subdirectory that you opened, you can return to the parent directory by selecting the "[...]" entry. To select a directory entry:

🖰 Double-click on it.

⌨ Use the cursor keys to highlight it and press <Enter>.

⑤ Select the "Add Icon" Button

🖰 Click on it.

⌨ Press <Alt> + <A>.

⑥ Select the "Done" Button

🖰 Click on it.

⌨ Press <Alt> + <D>.

Moving Icons

You move database icons by *dragging-and-dropping* with the mouse. You can even drag them to another Workspace page. To move an icon or icons, follow these steps:

1 Select the Icons

▶ To select a single icon, point at it, then press and hold the primary mouse button. Notes will depress the icon.

▶ To select multiple icons, press and hold the <Shift> key, then click on each icon. Notes will depress the selected icons. Point at any one of the icons, then press and hold the primary mouse button.

2 Drag the Icons

Drag the mouse toward the spot where you want to place the icon or icons. An empty white square or squares will appear under the cursor. To move the icons to a different page, drag them to the page's tab.

Database Icon in Transit (Example)

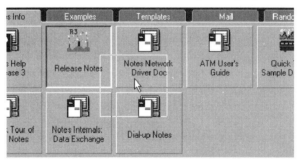

3 Drop the Icons

When the white square or squares are where you want the icon or icons to be, release the mouse button. To move the icons to a different page, place the cursor over the page's tab. When the tab's text has a box around it, release the mouse button.

Dropping on a Tab (Example)

Removing Icons

Removing an icon from the Workspace does <u>not</u> delete the underlying database. For help deleting a database, see page 33. To remove an icon or icons, follow these steps:

1 | Select the Icons

▶ To select a single icon, click on it. Notes will depress the icon.

▶ To select multiple icons, press and hold the <Shift> key, then click on each icon. Notes will depress the selected icons.

2 | Select the "Edit Clear" Command

🖱 Select "Clear" from the Edit menu. Click on "Edit" in the menu bar, then click on "Clear".

⌨ Press <Delete> or <Del>.

 Click on the Edit Clear SmartIcon.

You will receive a prompt something like this:

Remove Icons Prompt (Example)

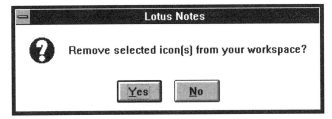

▶ Click on the Yes button or press <Y> to remove the icon or icons.

▶ Click on the No button or press <N> to leave the icon in place.

Creating a New Database

There are two ways to create a new database: you can use a template, which provides an off-the-shelf mock-up that you can modify to suit your needs; or you can work from scratch, building all of the database's elements yourself. You will probably not be surprised to learn that the latter approach is rather difficult and is beyond the scope of this book. To create a new database using a template, follow the steps below.

1 Decide Which Template You Want to Use

If you're creating a simple database for your own use, or to share with a few coworkers, one of Notes' standard templates will probably meet your needs. If not, ask your technical support person for help. The three most-likely-to-be-useful standard application templates are discussed below.

Storing & Handling Documents: Document Library Template

To create a database for collecting and manipulating documents, use the document library template. It's simple, straightforward, and flexible. One of the members of our editorial team uses a document library database as a repository and filter for documents that he downloads from the Internet. He dumps the document files into the database, then performs a full text search to find information that pertains to his specialties. (For help searching a database, see page 133.)

Communicating & Brainstorming: Discussion Template

To create a database for group discussions, or for personal brainstorming, use the discussion template. Its topic/response format is good for simple, open-ended discussions, or for recording your thoughts and ideas on a project that's in the drawing-board stages.

Coordinating: Things to Do Template

To keep yourself or a small group on track, use the Things to Do template. It uses a task/comment format that's good for developing and managing a project timeline.

2 Select a Workspace Page

Activate the Workspace window and select a page for the database's icon.

3 Access the "New Database" Dialog Box

Select "New Database" from the File menu. Click on "File" in the menu bar, then click on "New Database".

Press <Ctrl> + <N>.

Click on the File New Database SmartIcon.

New Database Dialog Box (Example)

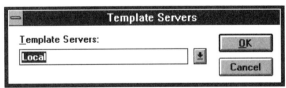

4 | Enter the Design Information

There are three Design settings: the template server, the template, and the Inherit Future Design Changes option.

Template Server

If you can't find the template that you want in the Template list box, try looking on a different server. Click on the Template Server button, or press <Alt> + <M>. Notes will open the Template Servers dialog box.

Template Servers Dialog Box

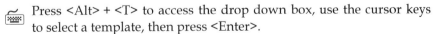

Use the drop down box to select a server, then select the OK button.

🖰 Open the drop down box by clicking on its Down Arrow button. Click on the server that you want to select, then click on the OK button.

⌨ Press <Alt> + <T> to access the drop down box, use the cursor keys to select a template, then press <Enter>.

Template

You can get information on a template by highlighting it in the Template list box and selecting the About button. To select a template:

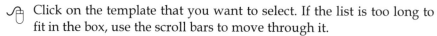 Click on the template that you want to select. If the list is too long to fit in the box, use the scroll bars to move through it.

Press <Alt> + <T> to access the list box. Use the cursor keys to highlight the template, or press the first character of the template's name until its list entry is highlighted.

Inherit Future Design Changes Option

If you select the Inherit Future Design Changes option, the new database will automatically be modified if any changes are made to the template. The option is on when the check box is filled. To turn it on or off:

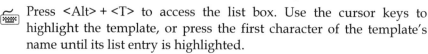 Click on the text or its check box.

Press <Alt> + <I>.

5 Enter the New Database Information

There are three New Database settings: the server, the file name, and the title.

Server

You select a server from the Server combo box.

Click on the server that you want to select. If the list is too long to fit in the box, use the scroll bars to move through it.

Press <Alt> + <T> to access the combo box, then press <↓> and/or < ↑> until the template is highlighted.

File Name

Enter the new database's file name in the File Name text box. The name cannot exceed eight characters. You do not have to add the ".NTF" file extension. To access the text box:

Click in it.

Press <Alt> + <F>.

Title

Enter the new database's title in the File Name text box. The name cannot exceed thirty-two characters. To access the text box:

Click in it.

Press <Alt> + <L>.

6 Select the "New" Button

🖰 Click on it.

⌨ Press <Alt> + <N>.

Notes will create the new database, add its icon to the Workspace page, and open the About Database document.

Deleting a Database

Deleting a database removes it permanently from your hard drive. To delete a database that is located on a server and not on your PC, you must have manager access to the database (see "Access Control Lists" on the following page). To delete a database or databases, follow the steps below.

1 Select the Icons

▶ To select a single icon, click on it. Notes will depress the icon.

▶ To select multiple icons, press and hold the <Shift> key, then click on each icon. Notes will depress the selected icons.

2 Select "Delete" from the "File Database" Sub-Menu

🖰 Click on "File" in the menu bar, click on "Database" in the File menu, then click on "Delete" in the sub-menu.

⌨ Press <Alt> + <F>, then <D>, then <D> again.

For each database that you selected, you will receive a prompt like this:

Delete Database Prompt (Example)

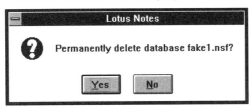

▶ Click on the Yes button or press <Y> to delete the database.

▶ Click on the No button or press <N> to leave the database as is.

Access Control Lists

Every database has an *Access Control List*. The list specifies which users can open the database and what tasks they can perform. The users can be defined individually, by user group, or by server.

Access Control Lists have two elements, *access levels* and *access roles*, both of which are set by the database's designer or its manager. Access levels (see table below) determine what operations can be performed by which users. Access roles determine which users have access to which forms or views. The symbol for your access level in the current database appears at the right end of the Status Bar (see page 13). See "Access Level Indicator" on page 16.

For more help with Access Control Lists, see Notes' on-line help, or speak with your technical support person. For help with on-line help, see "Using Notes Help" on page 177.

Access Levels		
Level	**Operations**	**Symbol**
Manager	All, including administrative tasks	☞
Designer	All, except administrative tasks	☞
Editor	Read, write, and edit all documents. Cannot modify forms, views, or the Access Control List.	☞
Author	Read and write documents. Edit documents they created.	☞
Reader	Read documents only	👓
Depositor	Write documents only. Typical uses: mail-in databases, ballot boxes, suggestion boxes.	🖨
No Access	None – cannot open the database or mail in documents	None

CHAPTER 4

Database Views

A *view* is a full or partial list of the database's documents, grouped and/or sorted according to pre-defined criteria. A database's views are designed by the database's creator.

Database View (Example)

Title	Created By...		Last Modified
HR Policies			
Holidays	01/21/93	Henri Paquard	01/21/93 12:46 PM
Sick Days	01/21/93	Gary Berkowitz	01/21/93 12:49 PM
Company-sponsored Sports Activities	01/21/93	Jose Guarenza	01/21/93 02:45 PM
Training Materials	01/21/93	Karen Leonard	01/21/93 12:59 PM
To do for next Review period	01/21/93	Karen Leonard	01/21/93 01:00 PM
Job Descriptions			
Systems Engineer	01/21/93	Jane Carlson	01/21/93 02:46 PM
Receptionist	01/21/93	Jose Guarenza	01/21/93 02:47 PM
Associate Buyer	01/21/93	Jose Guarenza	01/21/93 02:48 PM
I think we need to revise this job description (Karen Leonard)			
Office Services			
Use of Office Services	01/21/93	Gary Berkowitz	01/21/93 02:48 PM
Use of Bulletin Boards	01/21/93	Henri Paquard	01/21/93 02:49 PM

Notes' documentation likens views to tables of contents, but that's not entirely accurate: by definition, a table of contents includes everything in the given work, while views can include or exclude any or all of the database's documents. Each row in a view contains either a single document or a category heading. Each column contains one piece of information about the documents. For the user, views answer questions about the database. For example:

Question	Possible View
What documents are in here?	By Title
What are they about?	By Subject
Who wrote them?	By Author
When did they write them?	By Date and Time

Categories and Documents

A view either displays documents alone, or it displays categories and documents together. Categories alone are meaningless, since they're just a way of grouping documents. If a category doesn't contain any documents, Notes doesn't display the category. Categories usually appear flush left and documents are generally indented. A view that shows categories typically looks something like this:

```
Category 1
    Document
    Document
        Document
Category 2
    Document
    Document
```

Document Hierarchy

Documents that are indented further are affiliated with the preceding less-indented document. In Notes jargon, a top-level (least indented) document is called a *main document*, and documents that are affiliated with another document (more indented) are called *response documents*.

Main documents are so named because they are the top of the document heap. Response documents draw their name from their most common use: containing comments to another document. Returning to our example:

```
Category 1
    Main Document A
    Main Document B
        Response Document B1
Category 2
    Main Document C
    Main Document D
```

Response Documents

Response documents can have response documents of their own:

```
Category 1
    Main Document A
    Main Document B
        Response Document B1
            Response Document B1a
Category 2
    Main Document C
    Main Document D
```

Since a response document draws its meaning from the original document, the two are indelibly linked, with the response taking a subordinate role. Wherever goes the original document, hence goes its response documents. If someone reassigned Main Document B to Category 2, the display would change to something like this:

```
Category 1
    Main Document A
Category 2
    Main Document B
        Response Document B1
            Response Document B1a
    Main Document C
    Main Document D
```

And if someone deleted Main Document B, Notes would automatically delete any responses:

```
Category 1
    Main Document A
Category 2
    Main Document C
    Main Document D
```

Selecting a View

You change the view by choosing a new one from the bottom of the View menu.

 Click on "View" in the Menu Bar, then click on a view selection.

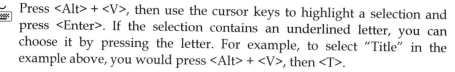 Press <Alt> + <V>, then use the cursor keys to highlight a selection and press <Enter>. If the selection contains an underlined letter, you can choose it by pressing the letter. For example, to select "Title" in the example above, you would press <Alt> + <V>, then <T>.

View SmartIcons

Notes has a set of SmartIcons for views. To use it, click on the SmartIcons button on the Status Bar (see page 13) and select "View Navigation" from the list. For help using SmartIcons, see "SmartIcons (Tool Bar)" on page 10. For help creating and editing sets of SmartIcons, see "Customizing Your SmartIcons" on page 169.

Getting Around

You may not be able to fit all of the view in the database window.

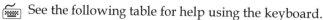 Use the scroll bars to scroll through the view. The scroll bars are relative: if you want to move halfway through the view, grab the vertical slider button and drag it halfway down the scroll bar. You highlight a row by clicking on it.

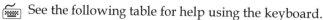 See the following table for help using the keyboard.

Views: Navigating with the Keyboard	
Movement / Location	**Keys**
Top of the view	<Ctrl> + <Home>
Bottom of the view	<Ctrl> + <End>
First column	<Home>
Last column	<End>
Next unread document	<Tab>
Previous unread document	<Shift> + <Tab>
Up one line	<↑>
Down one line	<↓>
Up one window	<Page Up>
Down one window	<Page Down>

Navigating with SmartIcons

The following table explains the SmartIcons that scan the view (see "View SmartIcons" on the preceding page).

Views: Navigating with SmartIcons	
	Moves to the next or previous main document. Skips responses and categories.
	Moves up or down one row. Doesn't skip anything.
	Moves to the next or previous unread document. Skips categories.
	Moves to the next or previous selected document or category. Doesn't skip anything.

Expanding and Contracting the View

> **Please Note:** There are three different versions of the View menu — one for database views, one for the Workspace, and one for documents. If the commands on your View menu vary from the discussion below, then the Workspace window or a document window must be active. Use the Window menu to select a database window.

The second section of the View menu contains commands for expanding and contracting the active view, so that the view includes more or less information. The following table outlines the commands, and a discussion follows.

Expanding and Contracting the View (Table I)			
View Menu Selection	**Shows**	**On/Off**	**Priority**
Expand All	All categories and documents		4
Collapse All	Top-level categories or main documents		2
Expand	Opens one level: shows sub-categories under current category, main documents under current category, or response documents under current document		5
Collapse	Closes one level: hides sub-categories under current category, main documents under current category, or response documents under current document		3
Show Only Unread	Documents which you have not opened, without categories	✓	1
Show Only Selected [1]	Selected categories and documents	✓	1
Show Only Categories	Categories only	✓	4
Show Only Search Results [2]	Documents that met search criteria	✓	1

---

[1] See "Selecting Documents" on page 119.

[2] See "Searching a Database" on page 133.

On/Off Commands

An on/off command has two states, on and off. When an on/off command is on, a check mark appears next to its menu selection. The first three on/off commands are

Turned On (Example)
√ **Show Only Unread**

mutually exclusive: turning on Show Only Unread, Show Only Categories, or Show Only Selected deactivates either of the other two.

Command Priority

The Priority Column (see table on the preceding page) indicates what ranking Notes assigns to each command, with one being the highest and five the lowest. For example, if you select Show Only Unread, followed by Expand All, the view will not change — the list of unread documents will remain on your screen — because Show Only Unread (1) has a higher priority than Expand All (4).

What happens in a tie? It depends. In the case of the three level 1 ranked commands, the odd ball is Show Only Search Results, the only non-mutually-exclusive toggle. Choosing it and one of the other two level 1 toggles will display the documents (not categories, since searches only look at documents) that are in both groups. For example, picking Show Only Selected and then Show Only Search Results, or vice-versa, will list all of the selected documents that met the search criteria.

Selecting a Command

The following table outlines the various methods for selecting the commands that expand and contract the view. To select one of the commands from the View menu:

 Click on "View" in the Menu Bar, then click on the selection.

 Press <Alt> + <V>, then use the cursor keys to highlight the selection and press <Enter>. If the selection contains an underlined letter, you can choose it by pressing the letter.

Expanding and Contracting the View (Table II)			
View Menu Selection	**SmartIcon**	**Hot Keys**	**Categories Only**
Expand All	⊞	<Shift>+<+>*	-None-
Collapse All	⊟	<Shift>+<->*	-None-
Expand	⊞	<+> or <*>	<Enter>, Double-Click
Collapse	⊟	<->	<Enter>, Double-Click
Show Only Unread	⯐ *	-None-	-None-
Show Only Selected	-None-	-None-	-None-
Show Only Categories	-None-	-None-	-None-
Show Only Search Results	-None-	-None-	-None-
* **Bug Alert:** The asterisked hot keys and SmartIcon do <u>not</u> work on the author's computer.			

Refreshing the View

If you make changes to a database, or are working on a database that someone else might be editing, you may want to update the view to reflect the changes. To refresh the view:

Refresh Panel

🖱 Click on the Refresh Panel.

🖱 Select "Refresh" from the View menu. Click on "View" in the Menu Bar, then click on "Refresh".

⌨ Press <F9>.

⚡ Click on the View Refresh Fields SmartIcon.

CHAPTER 5

Reading Documents

The typical Notes document is all or mostly text, but a document can also contain graphics, embedded files from other software packages, even multimedia elements.

Opening a Document

You open documents from database views. (For more help, see "Database Views" on page 35.)

Double-click on the document.

Use the cursor keys to highlight the document, then press <Enter>.

Notes will open a new *document window*. Document windows are secondary windows that display documents. (For more help, see "Manipulating Secondary Windows" on page 173.)

Document Window (Example)

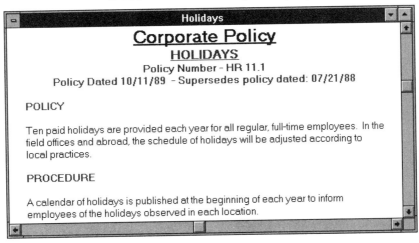

Getting Around

You may not be able to fit all of the document's text in the document window.

Use the scroll bars to scroll through the document. The scroll bars are relative: if you want to move halfway through the document, grab the vertical slider button and drag it halfway down the scroll bar.

See the following table for help using the keyboard.

Navigating with the Keyboard	
Movement / Location	**Keys**
Top of Document	<Ctrl> + <Home>
Bottom of Document	<Ctrl> + <End>
Left Edge	<Home>
Right Edge	<End>
Up One Line	<↑>
Down One Line	<↓>
Left One Character	<←>
Right One Character	<→>
Up One Pane	<Page Up>
Down One Pane	<Page Down>

Special Features

There are four special features than can be included in documents. These special features are discussed in detail below.

- **Attachments** (see the following page) are embedded files.
- **Buttons** (see page 47) look like the buttons that appear in dialog boxes.
- **Doclinks** (see page 47) do pretty much what the name says — link together two documents. They look like this: ▯.
- **Pop-Ups** (see page 48) provide a little extra information, typically definitions. A pop-up appears as text surrounded by a box.

Attachments

An attachment is an embedded file, represented by an icon and the file's name. If the file is associated with an application that has an icon, then Notes displays that application's icon. If not, Notes displays a generic icon that looks like a piece of paper with one corner folded down. An attachment's icon travels with the document, so you may see an icon for an application that is not on your system.

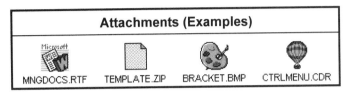

You can work with an attachment by opening the File Attachment Information dialog box, or you can select commands from the Edit Attachment sub-menu. The dialog box displays the file's name, its size ("length"), and its last-modified date and time. To open the dialog box:

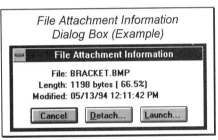

 Double-click on the attachment.

 Press <←> and/or <→> until the attachment is highlighted, then select "Information" from the Edit Attachment sub-menu. Press <Alt> + <E>, then <N>, then <I>.

▶ *Saving the Attachment*

To save the attachment as an independent file, click on the Detach button, or press <D>. Notes will open the Save Attachment dialog box (see "Saving an Attachment" on the following page). You can also access the Save Attachment dialog box by selecting "Detach" from the Edit Attachment sub-menu.

▶ *Opening or Running the Attachment*

To open or run the file in its native application, click on the Launch button, or press <L>. This is the same as selecting "Launch" from the Edit Attachment sub-menu. If the application is not on your system, you will receive a message telling you so.

▶ *Closing the Dialog Box*

To close the dialog box, click on the Cancel button, or press <Esc>.

Saving an Attachment

When you choose to detach an attachment, Notes opens the Save Attachment dialog box. To close the dialog box without detaching the file, click on the Cancel button or press <Esc>. To save the attachment, follow the steps below.

Save Attachment Dialog Box (Example)

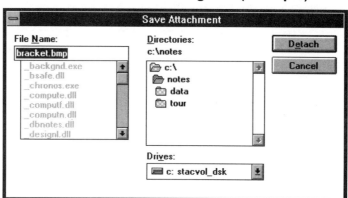

1 Enter the File Name (Optional)

Notes automatically enters the current file name into the File Name text box. You can enter a new name by typing over this text. Don't forget the file extension, which is the period and subsequent letters at the end of the file's name. In the example above it's ".bmp". To access the text box:

 Double-click in it to overwrite the current text, or click in it to edit the current text.

Press <Alt> + <N>.

2 Select the Path

You select the path by selecting a drive and a directory.

Selecting a Disk Drive

You change the disk drive from the Drive drop down box.

Drive Drop Down Box (Example)

Click on the drop down box to open it, then click on the drive that you want. If the list is too long to fit in the box, use the scroll bar to move through it.

Press <Alt> + <V> and then <↓> to open the drop down box. Press the drive letter and then <Enter>.

Selecting a Directory

You change the directory from the Directories list box. To reach a subdirectory you must first select its parent directory. To select a directory:

Directories List
Box (Example)

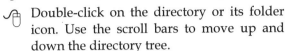 Double-click on the directory or its folder icon. Use the scroll bars to move up and down the directory tree.

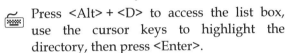 Press <Alt> + <D> to access the list box, use the cursor keys to highlight the directory, then press <Enter>.

3 Select the "Detach" Button

Click on it.

Press <Alt> + <E>.

Buttons

The buttons in documents look and behave like those that appear in all Windows dialog boxes. A button performs a Notes command or other action; the button's text should give some indication what that command or action is. To activate a button:

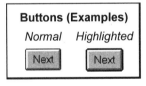

Buttons (Examples)
Normal   Highlighted

Click on it.

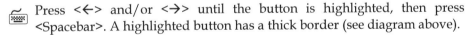 Press <←> and/or <→> until the button is highlighted, then press <Spacebar>. A highlighted button has a thick border (see diagram above).

Doclinks

A doclink provides quick access to a related document. A doclink usually appears immediately after some word or phrase that is explained or elaborated upon in the linked document. You can find

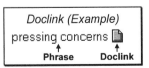

Doclink (Example)
pressing concerns
Phrase   Doclink

out where the doclink goes by pointing at it with the mouse and pressing and holding the primary mouse button:

To activate a doclink:

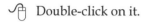 Double-click on it.

Press <←> and/or <→> until it's highlighted, then press <Spacebar>. A highlighted doclink has a box around it, like this:

Pop-Ups

Pop-ups provide a little extra information, typically definitions. A pop-up usually appears as text surrounded by a box. Notes' documentation states that the color of pop-up boxes is green on color monitors, but some users report the color as brown. When you activate a pop-up, Notes displays a "floating" box that contains text:

Pop-Up
(Example)
flunkie

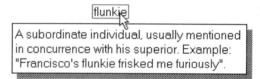

To activate a pop-up:

Point at it with the mouse, then press and hold the primary mouse button.

> **Bug Alert!** The following keyboard instructions come directly from
> ☠ Notes' documentation. We couldn't get them to work.

Press <←> and/or <→> until the cursor appears within the box, then press <Spacebar>. Press <Spacebar> again to close the pop-up.

Searching for Text

> **Tip:** You can also search for text within an entire database. See "Searching a Database" on page 133.

To search for text within the active document, follow these steps:

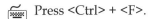 **1** ## Select Text to Find (Optional)

As far as can be determined, this is an undocumented feature: if there is text selected in the document when you access the Find and Replace dialog box (see next step), Notes loads the selected text into the dialog box. If you want to find the next occurrence of some word or phrase that is right in front of you, select it now. See "Selecting Text with the Mouse" on page 61 or "Selecting Text with the Keyboard" on page 61.

2 ## Access the "Find and Replace" Dialog Box

Select "Find & Replace" from the Edit menu. Click on "Edit" in the menu bar, then click on "Find & Replace".

Press <Ctrl> + <F>.

Click on the Edit Find SmartIcon.

Find and Replace Dialog Box

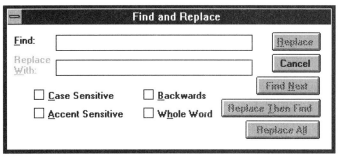

3 ## Enter the Text (Optional)

If you didn't select text in Step 1, you have to enter text now. Type it into the Find text box. You can enter special characters (see page 82). To access the text box:

Double-click in it to overwrite the current text (if any), or click in it to edit the current text.

Press <Alt> + <F>.

4 | Set the Search Options

There are four search options, each of which are explained below. You turn an option on or off by clicking on its label or its check box, or by pressing <Alt> plus the option's underlined letter.

- **Case Sensitive**
  When the check box is filled, Notes searches for text with identical capitalization. For example, Notes will ignore "fungus" when searching for "Fungus".

- **Accent Sensitive**
  When the check box is filled, Notes searches for text with identical accents. For example, Notes will ignore "ano" when searching for "año".

- **Backwards**
  When the check box is filled, Notes searches toward the beginning of the document. Otherwise, Notes searches toward the end.

- **Whole Word**
  When the check box is filled, Notes ignores text if it is partly or entirely contained within another word. For example, Notes will ignore "shipping" when searching for "ship".

5 | Select the "Find Next" Button

Click on it.

Press <Alt> + <N>.

6 | Keep Searching (Optional)

There are two ways you can keep searching: you can select the Find Next button again, or you can close the dialog box and use the Edit Find Next command.

Select "Find Next" from the Edit menu. Click on "Edit" in the menu bar, then click on "Find Next".

Press <Ctrl> + <G>.

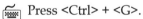 Click on the Edit Find Again SmartIcon.

Paging Through the Database

The SmartIcons that you can use to scan a view also work from a document window, with similar results. The following table outlines these SmartIcons.

SmartIcons: Scanning the Database	
🔽🔼	Moves to the next or previous main document. Skips responses.
🔽🔼	Moves up or down one document.
⭐🔽⭐🔼	Moves to the next or previous unread document.
✓🔽✓🔼	Moves to the next or previous selected document.

If Notes finds a document that meets the SmartIcon's criteria, it closes the current document and opens the new one. If no documents meet the criteria, Notes closes the document window and activates the most recently active window. In most cases, this will be the view from which you opened the first document.

Printing the Active Document

Tip: You can't select a printer from the dialog box that you use to print documents. For help selecting a printer, see page 168.

To print the document that you are currently viewing, follow these steps:

1 Access the "File Print" Dialog Box

🖰 Select "Print" from the File menu. Click on "File" in the menu bar, then click on "Print".

⌨ Press <Ctrl> + <P>.

🖨 Click on the File Print SmartIcon.

File Print Dialog Box

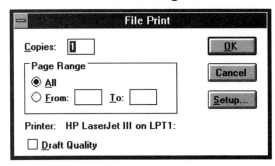

2 Set the Number of Copies

Enter the number of copies you want to print in the Copies text box. To access the text box:

🖱 Double-click in it to overwrite the current number. Click in it to edit.

⌨ Press <Alt> + <C>.

3 Set the Page Range

You set the page range from the Page Range group box. To print the entire document, click on the All option, or press <Alt> + <A>. To print a range of pages by page number:

① Click on the From option button, or press <Alt> + <F>. Notes will fill the option button.

② Enter the starting page in the From text box. To access the text box, click in it, or press <Tab>.

③ Enter the ending page in the To text box. To access the text box, click in it, or press <Tab> or <Alt> + <T>.

4 Set the "Draft Quality" Option

On most printers, documents print faster with the Draft Quality option on, but the output doesn't look as good. To turn the option on:

🖱 Click on "Draft Quality" or on the small box next to it.

⌨ Press <Alt> + <D>.

5 Select the "OK" Button

To send the document to the printer, click on the OK button, or press <Alt> + <O>. To close the dialog box without printing the document, click on the Cancel button, or press <Esc>.

Closing the Active Document

You close a document by closing its window, which is the same process as closing any other secondary window:

 Select "Close Window" from the File menu. Click on "File" in the menu bar, then click on "Close Window".

 Double-click on the window's Control box (▣).

 Double-click in the window with the secondary mouse button.

 Press <Esc>.

 Press <Ctrl> + <W>.

 Press <Ctrl> + <F4>.

CHAPTER 6

Editing Documents

> **Important!** In order to create and edit documents, your access level for the database must be author or higher. For more information, see "Access Control Lists" on page 34.

Documents and Fields

Documents consist of *fields*. A field is the space that is set aside for a certain piece of information. A simple document might consist of a field for the title, a field for the author, and a field for the document's body.

In some databases all of the documents are alike, meaning that they all have the same fields. Other databases contain documents with very different field structures. For example, a database that tracks customer contacts and orders might contain three types of documents: customer profiles, contact reports, and product orders.

Getting Help with Fields

You can tell Notes to display a brief description of the active field at the bottom of the document's window.

Field Help (Example)

Categories that apply to this document – press Enter for choices.

To turn field help on or off, you select "Show Field Help" from the View menu.

Click on "View" in the menu bar, then click on "Show Field Help".

Press <Alt> + <V>, then <F>.

Text Fields: Plain Vs. Rich

Text fields come in two varieties, *plain text* and *rich text*. The basic editing commands that you use in both types of text fields are explained in the next section (see "Basic Editing Commands" on page 60).

Plain Text Fields

All you can do in a plain text field is add and remove characters. When you're in a plain text field, the typeface indicator and point size indicator on the Status Bar (see page 13) are blank.

Rich Text Fields

Rich text fields accept text formatting, paragraph formatting, special characters, tables, OLE objects, and Notes special document features (doclinks, pop-ups, buttons, and attachments). When you're in a rich text field, Notes displays the current typeface and point size on the Status Bar (see page 13).

- ▶ For help with attachments, doclinks, imported files, OLE objects, pop-ups, special characters, and tables, see "Editing Rich Text" on page 67.
- ▶ For help applying fonts to text and formatting paragraphs, see "Formatting Rich Text" on page 99.

Edit Document SmartIcons

Notes has a set of SmartIcons for editing documents. To use it, click on the SmartIcons button on the Status Bar (see page 13), and select "Edit Document" from the list. For help using SmartIcons, see "SmartIcons (Tool Bar)" on page 10.

> **Please Note:** This chapter mentions SmartIcons that do not appear in the Edit Document set. For help creating and editing sets of SmartIcons, see "Customizing Your SmartIcons" on page 169.

Creating a New Document

You can create a new document from a view, from another document, or from a database's icon in the Workspace. To create a new document, follow these steps:

1 Select the View, Icon, or Document

Where you are can determine what types of documents you can create. For example, in a database that has main documents and response documents, you can only create a response document from an open main document or from a view with a main document highlighted. You cannot create a response document from a database's icon because Notes can't tell which main document you want to respond to.

Selecting a View

If the database is open, make sure its window is active. You select a window from the bottom section of the Windows menu. If the database isn't open, open it now. Select the view that you want to use. If you want to create a document that is based on or in response to another document, highlight the "parent" document.

Selecting a Database Icon

If the Workspace isn't active, select it now. You can select the Workspace from the bottom section of the Windows menu, or if it's available, by clicking on the Workspace SmartIcon. Highlight the icon for the database that you want to use.

Selecting a Document

If the document is open, make sure its window is active. You select a window from the bottom section of the Windows menu. If the document isn't open, open it now.

2 Select a Form

A *form* is a template that contains the necessary fields for a certain type of document. You use a form as the basis for a new document. You select a form from the Compose menu.

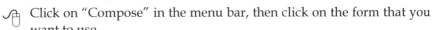 Click on "Compose" in the menu bar, then click on the form that you want to use.

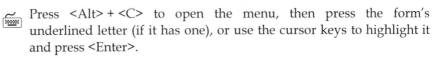 Press <Alt> + <C> to open the menu, then press the form's underlined letter (if it has one), or use the cursor keys to highlight it and press <Enter>.

> **Tip:** When you create a new document, it might copy some of its values from the document that is currently highlighted in the database view. To prevent this, hold down <Ctrl> while you click on the form in the Compose menu. You cannot use this feature with the keyboard.

Notes will open a new document based on the form.

New Document (Example)

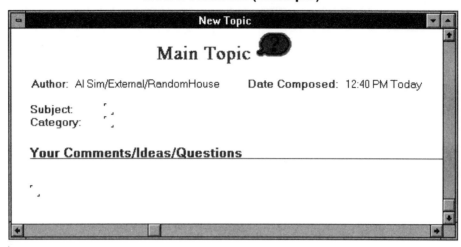

3 Enter Some Text

The new document will be in *edit mode*, which means that you can edit the contents of some or all of the document's fields. When a document is in edit mode, you can see brackets at the beginning and end of each *editable field*. An editable field is exactly that, a field that you can edit. In the example above, there are three editable fields: subject, category, and the document's body, which appears under the heading "Your Comments/Ideas/Questions".

For now, don't worry about creating the entire document — you'll get help with that in later sections of this chapter and in subsequent chapters. Just enter something in the editable fields. You can move from field to field using the cursor keys, or you can click in the field that you want to fill.

4 Save the Document

 Click on "File" in the menu bar, then click on "Save". If it's available, you can click on the File Save SmartIcon instead.

Press <Ctrl> + <S>.

Click on the File Save SmartIcon.

Some document types have *required fields*, which must be filled in before you can save the document. In the example above, the only required field is the subject. If you try to save a document without having filled each of the required fields, you will receive an error message.

Employee Communications

09/09/96 10:06:33 AM

To: SMS Notes Users - Q, SMS Notes Users - R, SMS Notes Users - S, SMS Notes Users - T, SMS Notes Users - U, SMS Notes Users - V, SMS Notes Users - W, SMS Notes Users - X, SMS Notes Users - Y, SMS Notes Users - Z

cc:

Subject: ASAP Online Reminder

Don't forget to check *ASAP Online* this morning!

Remember, it's time to check *ASAP Online*! You can stay up-to-date by checking the database for news, events, and other important information every Monday.

We've received lots of positive feedback and hope you'll continue to provide us with suggestions and feedback via the "Submit Article" button (or by sending an e-mail to "ASAP").

Simple instructions to access the database*:
1. Sign on to Lotus Notes.
2. Under the menu bar at the top, select "File."
3. Select "Database" then "Open" (if you're running Notes 4.0. If you're running an earlier version, you'll need to select "Open" then "Database.")
4. Under "server, " select Jupiter. If you can't view Jupiter, select SMS_IOS.
5. Scroll the menu bar down to view items on the server, and find the "General Interest" folder. Double click on the folder.
6. Double click on *ASAP Online*, and the database icon will be added to your desktop.
7. Double click on the icon to view items in the database. Items are separated into Field and Malvern-area announcements for easy viewing.
8. Check it every Monday for the week's information.
9. Let us know how you like it! Use the "Submit Article" button to give us feedback.

* *MS4 employees have access to the database through their division server. See Beth Gardiner for more info.*

QUESTIONS??? Contact Employee Communications at x4930.

Required Field Error Message (Example)

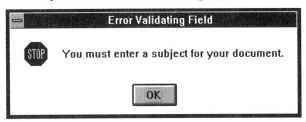

Click on the OK button to close the error message, or press <Enter>, <Esc>, or <Spacebar>. Fill the required fields and try again.

Putting a Document in Edit Mode

You put a document in *edit mode* so that you can edit the contents of some or all of the document's fields. When a document is in edit mode, you can see brackets at the beginning and end of each *editable field*. An editable field is (no surprise) a field that you can edit. Follow these steps:

1 Select the Document

If the document is closed, highlight its row in a view. If the document is open, select its window from the bottom section of the Window menu.

Click on "Window" in the menu bar, then click on the window's name.

Press <Alt> + <W>, then press the underlined number that appears before the window's name.

2 Select the Edit Document Command

Select "Edit Document" from the Edit menu.

Press <Ctrl> + <E>.

Click on the Edit Document SmartIcon.

Basic Editing Commands

The following five sections outline Notes' fundamental editing commands.

▶ For help positioning the insertion point, see below.

▶ For help selecting text with the mouse, see the following page.

▶ For help selecting text with the keyboard, see the following page.

▶ For help cutting and pasting, see page 62.

▶ For help with the Edit Undo command, see page 62.

Positioning the Insertion Point

To place the insertion point in a field, click where you want it to be. Use the scroll bars to scroll through the document. The scroll bars are relative: if you want to move halfway through the document, grab the vertical slider button and drag it halfway down the scroll bar.

See the following table for help using the keyboard.

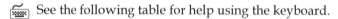 Positioning the Insertion Point		
Movement / Location	**Field Types**	**Keys**
New Paragraph	Both	<Enter>
First Editable Field	Both	<Ctrl> + <Home>
Last Editable Field	Both	<Ctrl> + <End>
Next Tab Stop	Rich Text	<Tab>
Previous Tab Stop	Rich Text	<Backspace>
Next Field	Plain Text	<Tab>
Previous Field	Plain Text	<Shift> + <Tab>
Word Right	Both	<Ctrl> + <→>
Word Left	Both	<Ctrl> + <←>
Up One Line	Both	<↑>
Down One Line	Both	<↓>
Left One Character	Both	<←>
Right One Character	Both	<→>

Selecting Text with the Mouse

There are four ways to select text with the mouse.

 Dragging the Insertion Point

① Point at the spot where you want the selection to begin

② Press and hold the primary mouse button

③ Drag the insertion point to the end of the text

 Click Followed by <Shift> + Click

① Click at the spot where you want the selection to begin

② Press and hold the <Shift> key

③ Click at the spot where you want the selection to end

 Double-Click

To select a single word, double-click on it.

 Edit Select All / Edit Deselect All

To select the entire contents of the current field, select "Select All" from the Edit menu, or click on the Select All SmartIcon. To deselect the field, select "Deselect All" from the Edit menu.

Selecting Text with the Keyboard

The following table outlines the ways to select text with the keyboard.

⌨ Selecting Text	
Extend Selection To	**Keys**
Character Right	<Shift> + <→>
Character Left	<Shift> + <←>
Word Right	<Ctrl> + <Shift> + <→>
Word Left	<Ctrl> + <Shift> + <←>
End of Line	<Shift> + <End>
Beginning of Line	<Shift> + <Home>
Entire Field	<Ctrl> + <A>

Cutting and Pasting

You use the Windows Clipboard to cut and paste text or other data. The following table explains the cut and paste commands and gives keyboard and mouse instructions.

Cutting and Pasting in a Document					
Command	**Selection Effect**	**Clipboard Effect**	**Keys**	**Edit Menu Selection**	**SmartIcon**
Cut	Clears selection	Replaces contents with selection	\<Ctrl\> + \<X\>	"Cut"	✂
Copy	-None-	Replaces contents with selection	\<Ctrl\> + \<C\>	"Copy"	🅰
Append	-None-	Adds selection to end of contents	\<Ctrl\> + \<Shift\> + \<Insert\>	-None-	-None-
Paste	Clears any selected text and inserts Clipboard contents	-None-	\<Ctrl\> + \<V\>	"Paste"	📋
Clear	Deletes selection	-None-	\<Delete\>	"Clear"	🗑

Edit Undo

The Edit Undo command undoes your last text entry, command, or other action. The command is the first selection on the Edit menu, but its name depends on your last action: if you copied something, it's Undo Copy; if you deleted something it's Undo Delete; etc. If the last thing that you did is not "undo-able", then Notes dims the Undo selection. To undo something:

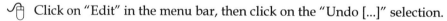 Click on "Edit" in the menu bar, then click on the "Undo [...]" selection.

 Press \<Ctrl\> + \<Z\>.

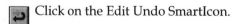 Click on the Edit Undo SmartIcon.

Headers and Footers

Headers and footers appear at the top and bottom respectively of each printed page. You create and edit headers and footers from the Edit Header/Footer dialog box. To access the dialog box, select "Header/Footer" from the Edit menu.

 Click on "Edit" in the menu bar, then click on "Header/Footer".

Press <Alt> + <E>, then <H>.

Click on the Edit Header Footer SmartIcon.

Edit Header/Footer Dialog Box

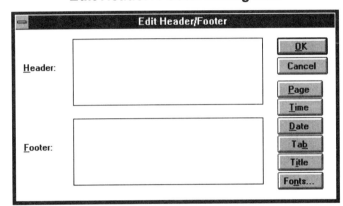

You create a header or footer by entering text and/or special markers into the appropriate text box. You access a text box by clicking in it or pressing <Alt> plus the underlined letter. You enter the markers by selecting one of the five buttons outlined in the table below. The Fonts button accesses the Font dialog box (see page 100), which you can use to format the header or footer's text.

Headers and Footers: Inserting Markers		
Button	**Marker**	**Description**
Page	&P	Page number
Time	&T	Time of printing
Date	&D	Date of printing
Tab	|	Positions text to left, center, or right. See the following page.
Title	&W	Window title, usually the name of the document

Tab Stops

There are three tab stops in headers and footers — left, center, and right. Their locations cannot be changed, and new stops cannot be added.

▶ When you insert <u>one</u> tab, everything to the left of the tab is left-justified, and everything to its right is right-justified.

▶ With <u>two</u> tabs, everything to the left of the first tab is left-justified, everything between the two tabs is centered, and everything to the right of the second tab is right-justified.

Header and Footer Tab Stops (Examples)	
Example	**Description**
&D &T	Left-justifies the date and time
Draft #1|&P	Left-justifies "Draft #1" and right-justifies the page number
&D &T|&W|&P	Left-justifies the date and time, centers the title, and right-justifies the page number
|Urgent!!!|	Centers "Urgent!!!"
|&P	Right-justifies the page number

Checking Your Spelling

To perform a spell check, start by putting the document in edit mode (see page 59). Select the text that you want to check, or don't select any text if you want to check the entire document. Select "Spell Check" from the Tools menu.

 Click on "Tools" in the menu bar, then click on "Spell Check".

 Press <Alt> + <O>, then <K>.

Click on the Tools Spell Check SmartIcon.

If Notes doesn't find any misspelled words, you'll receive a prompt telling you so. If there are misspelled words, Notes will open the Tools Check Spelling dialog box.

No Misspellings Prompt

Tools Check Spelling Dialog Box (Example)

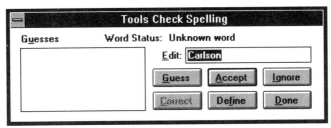

You can change the selected text by editing it in the Edit text box. For help with the dialog box's buttons, see the following table. To select one of the buttons, click on it, or press <Alt> plus the button's underlined letter.

Tools Check Spelling Dialog Box Buttons	
Button	**Explanation**
Accept	Accepts the word as correct and ignores any other occurrences of it.
Correct	Replaces the word with the selected word in the Guesses list box (see Guess below) or with the corrected word in the Edit text box.
Define	Adds the word to your user dictionary, where it will be available to check subsequent words and for future spell checks.
Done	Closes the dialog box.
Guess	Lists potential spellings in the Guesses list box. To use one of the words, highlight it and select the Correct button.
Ignore	Leaves this occurrence of the word alone. Any subsequent occurrences will be considered misspelled.

Saving Your Changes

> **Tip:** Don't limit your frequent saves to your work in Notes! If it's time to save your Notes work, it's also time to save anything you're working on in any other application. If Notes goes down, chances are it'll take everything else with it.

It's always a good idea to save your work frequently. With Windows and Notes combined, it's an even better idea, since Notes seems to decrease Windows' stability. You may find that some or all of your other Windows applications are less stable when Notes is running.

To save a Notes document:

Select "Save" from the File menu. Click on "File" in the menu bar, then click on "Save".

Press <Ctrl> + <S>.

Click on the File Save SmartIcon.

Some document types have *required fields,* which must be filled in before you can save the document. If you try to save a document without having filled each of the required fields, you will receive an error message.

Required Field Error Message (Example)

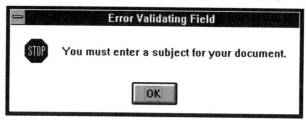

Click on the OK button to close the error message, or press <Enter>, <Esc>, or <Spacebar>. Fill the required fields and try again.

CHAPTER 7

Editing Rich Text

Rich text fields accept text formatting (fonts), paragraph formatting, imported files, OLE objects, special characters, tables, and Notes' special document features (doclinks, pop-ups, buttons, and attachments). This chapter covers:

- Attachments (see below)
- Doclinks (see page 70)
- Importing a File (see page 72)
- OLE Objects (see page 74)
- Pop-Ups (see page 79)
- Resizing a Picture (see page 81)
- Special Characters (see page 82)
- Tables (see pages 89 and 94)

Creating a button requires a fairly advanced knowledge of Notes and is beyond the scope of this book.

> **Please Note:** This chapter mentions SmartIcons that do not appear in the Edit Document set. For help creating and editing sets of SmartIcons, see "Customizing Your SmartIcons" on page 169.

Attachments

An attachment is an embedded file, represented by an icon and the file's name. If the file is associated with an application that has an icon, then Notes displays that application's icon. If not, Notes displays a generic icon that looks like a piece of paper with one corner folded down. An attachment's icon travels with the document, so you may see an icon for an application that is not on your system.

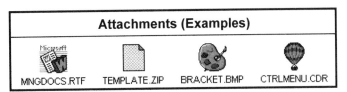

Attachments (Examples)

MNGDOCS.RTF   TEMPLATE.ZIP   BRACKET.BMP   CTRLMENU.CDR

To create an attachment (or attachments), follow these steps:

1 **Position the Insertion Point**

Place the insertion point where you want to insert the attachment. For help, see "Positioning the Insertion Point" on page 60.

2 **Access the "Insert Attachment(s)" Dialog Box**

Select "Attach" from the File menu.

🖰 Click on "File" in the menu bar, then click on "Attach".

⌨ Press <Alt> + <F>, then <A>.

📎 Click on the Edit Insert Attachment SmartIcon.

Insert Attachment(s) Dialog Box

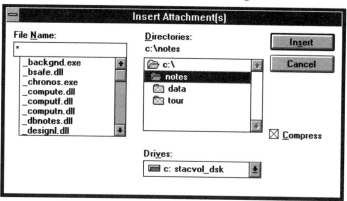

> **Bug Alert!** Notes' on-line help says that the Insert Attachment(s) dialog box has a List Files of Type drop down box. We can't find it.

3 **Select the Path**

You select the path by selecting a drive and a directory.

Selecting a Disk Drive

You change the disk drive from the Drive drop down box.

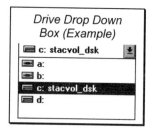

Drive Drop Down Box (Example)

🖰 Click on the drop down box to open it, then click on the drive that you want. If the list is too long to fit in the box, use the scroll bars to move through it.

⌨ Press <Alt> + <V> and then <↓> to open the drop down box. Press the drive letter and then <Enter>.

Selecting a Directory

You change the directory from the Directories list box. To reach a subdirectory you must first select its parent directory. To select a directory:

Directories List
Box (Example)

 Double-click on the directory or its folder icon. Use the scroll bars to move up and down the directory tree.

 Press <Alt> + <D> to access the list box, use the cursor keys to highlight the directory, then press <Enter>.

4 Select the Files

You can create more than one attachment at a time. You select the files that you want to attach from the list section of the File Name combo box. To select a single file:

Click on it. If the list doesn't fit in the box, use the scroll bars to move through it.

 To access the list section of the combo box, press <Alt> + <N>, then <Tab> once. Use the cursor keys to highlight the file.

Selecting Files In Sequence

To select files in sequence, click on the first file, then hold down the <Shift> key and click on the last file. All of the files between your two selections will be selected.

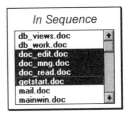

In Sequence

Selecting Files Out of Sequence

To select files out of sequence, hold down the <Ctrl> key while you click on the files that you want.

Narrowing the File List

You can narrow the file list by typing characters in the text section of the combo box, and then pressing <Enter>. An asterisk ("*") equals any group of characters, and a question mark ("?") equals any single character. To see only those files with a certain file extension, enter "*" plus the extension. (For example, to see text files, enter "*.TXT".) To access the text section of the combo box:

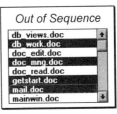

Out of Sequence

Double-click in it to overwrite the text. Click in it once to edit.

 Press <Alt> + <N>.

5 | Set the "Compress" Option

The Compress Option is on by default. When it's on, Notes compresses the files. To turn the option on or off:

🖰 Click on the label or the check box.

⌨ Press \<Alt> + \<C>.

6 | Select the "Insert" Button

🖰 Click on it.

⌨ Press \<Alt> + \<S>.

Notes will insert the files and display their names and icons.

Buttons

The buttons in documents look and behave like those that appear in all Windows dialog boxes. Creating a button requires a fairly advanced knowledge of Notes and is beyond the scope of this book. For help creating a button, refer to your Notes documentation or Notes' on-line help (see "Using Notes Help" on page 177).

Button
(Example)

Doclinks

A doclink provides quick access to a related document. A doclink usually appears immediately after some word or phrase that is explained or elaborated upon in the linked document. Creating a doclink is extremely easy — just follow these simple steps:

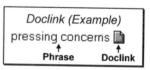

Doclink (Example)

pressing concerns 📄

Phrase   Doclink

1 | Access the "Jump To" Document

The "Jump To" document is the document that the doclink takes the reader to. It does <u>not</u> have to be open — you can simply highlight its row in a view (see "Getting Around" on page 38).

2 Start the Doclink

Select "Make DocLink" from the Edit menu.

🖱 Click on "Edit" in the menu bar, then click on "Make DocLink".

⌨ Press <Alt> + <E>, then <M>.

🔲 Click on the Edit Make Doc Link SmartIcon.

If you were successful, Notes displays the following message in the Status Bar:

DocLink copied to clipboard. Use Paste to insert it into a document.

3 Access the "Jump From" Document

The "Jump From" document is the document that the reader starts from. If the "Jump From" document is open but not active, select its entry from the Window menu. If the document isn't open, open it in Edit Mode (see "Putting a Document in Edit Mode" on page 59).

4 Put the "Jump From" Document in Edit Mode

If the "Jump From" document isn't in Edit Mode, turn it on now. See "Putting a Document in Edit Mode" on page 59.

5 Position the Insertion Point

Place the insertion point where you want to insert the doclink. For help, see "Positioning the Insertion Point" on page 60.

6 Paste It In

🖱 Select "Paste" from the Edit menu. Click on "Edit" in the menu bar, then click on "Paste".

⌨ Press <Ctrl> + <V>.

🔲 Click on the Edit Paste SmartIcon.

Importing a File

You can import a variety of file formats into a Notes document. For example, you can use a graphics application to create a picture, then import the picture's file into a document. To import a file, follow these steps:

1 Position the Insertion Point

Place the insertion point where you want to insert the file. For help, see "Positioning the Insertion Point" on page 60.

2 Access the "Import" Dialog Box

Select "Import" from the File menu.

🖰 Click on "File" in the menu bar, then click on "Import".

⌨ Press <Alt> + <F>, then <I>.

📲 Click on the File Import SmartIcon.

Import Dialog Box

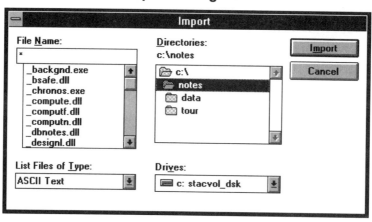

3 Select the Path

You select the path by selecting a drive and a directory.

Selecting a Disk Drive

You change the disk drive from the Drive drop down box.

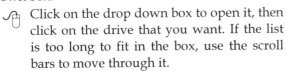

Drive Drop Down Box (Example)

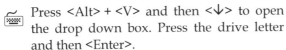

Click on the drop down box to open it, then click on the drive that you want. If the list is too long to fit in the box, use the scroll bars to move through it.

Press <Alt> + <V> and then <↓> to open the drop down box. Press the drive letter and then <Enter>.

Selecting a Directory

You change the directory from the Directories list box. To reach a subdirectory you must first select its parent directory. To select a directory:

Directories List Box (Example)

Double-click on the directory or its folder icon. Use the scroll bars to move up and down the directory tree.

Press <Alt> + <D> to access the list box, use the cursor keys to highlight the directory, then press <Enter>.

4 Select the File Type

You select a file type from the List Files of Type drop down box.

List Files of Type Drop Down Box

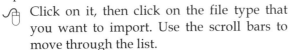

Click on it, then click on the file type that you want to import. Use the scroll bars to move through the list.

Press <Alt> + <T>. Keep pressing the first character of the file type until it is highlighted, or use the cursor keys to move through the list. Press <Enter>.

5 Select the File

You select the file from the list section of the File Name combo box. The selected file appears in the combo box's text section.

Click on the file. If the entire list doesn't fit in the box, use the scroll bars to move through it.

To access the list section, Press <Alt> + <N>, then press <Tab> once. Press the first character of the file's name until it is highlighted, or highlight it with the cursor keys.

Narrowing the File List

You can narrow the file list by typing characters in the text section of the combo box, and then pressing <Enter>. An asterisk ("*") equals any group of characters, and a question mark ("?") equals any single character. To see only those files with a certain file extension, enter "*" plus the extension. (For example, to see text files, enter "*.TXT".) To access the text section:

    Double-click in it to overwrite the text. Click in it once to edit.

    Press <Alt> + <N>.

6 Select the "Import" Button

    Click on it.

    Press <Alt> + <M>.[1]

Notes will close the Import dialog box and insert the selected file.

OLE Objects

OLE (Object Linking and Embedding) is Windows' protocol for sharing data between applications and for creating compound files. An OLE object is a file created in another application and stored within a Notes document. This section explains two ways of creating an OLE object: by creating a new file from scratch, and by embedding a copy of an existing file.

Creating an OLE Object

To create an OLE object, follow the steps below. The first four steps are identical whether you're creating a new object or selecting an existing file; after that, they diverge.

1 Position the Insertion Point

Place the insertion point where you want to insert the object. For help, see "Positioning the Insertion Point" on page 60.

---

[1] In several places, Notes uses hot keys that are not the obvious choice. Here, for example, Notes could have used <Alt> + <I>.

2 Access the "Insert Object" Dialog Box

To access the Insert Object dialog box, select "Object" from the Edit Insert sub-menu.

Click on "Edit" in the menu bar, click on "Insert" in the Edit menu, then click on "Object" in the sub-menu.

Press <Alt> + <E>, then <I>, and then <O>.

Click on the Edit Insert Object SmartIcon.

Insert Object Dialog Box

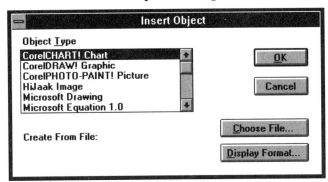

3 Select the Object Type

You select the object type from the Object Type list box.

Click on it. Use the scroll bars to move through the list.

Press <Alt> + <T> to access the list box. Press the first character of the object type until it is highlighted, or use the cursor keys to move through the list.

4 Select the Display Format

You select the display format from the Insert Object Display Format dialog box.

Click on the Display Format button to open the dialog box, then double-click on the format that you want to select.

Press <Alt> + <D> to open the dialog box, use the cursor keys to highlight the format, then press <Alt> + <O>.

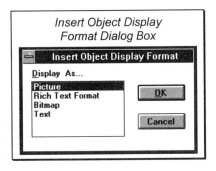

Insert Object Display Format Dialog Box

> **Please Note:**
> ▶ To create a **new object**, continue at "Creating an OLE Object from Scratch" (see below).
> ▶ To copy an **existing file**, continue at "Creating an OLE Object from an Existing File" (see below).

⇒ Creating an OLE Object from Scratch

When you create a new file from scratch, it is stored within the Notes document. No external version of the file is created. Continuing with our steps:

5 Select the "OK" Button

🖱 Click on it.

⌨ Press <Alt> + <O>.

6 Create the Object

Here you're on your own, with one little tip: to send your work back to Notes, select "Update" from the other application's File menu.

⇒ Creating an OLE Object from an Existing File

When you create an object by copying an existing file, you are embedding the copy within the Notes document. There is no link between the original file and the object in Notes. Continuing with our steps:

5 Select the "Choose File" Button

🖱 Click on it.

⌨ Press <Alt> + <C>.

Notes will open the Insert Object Choose File dialog box.

Insert Object Choose File Dialog Box

Insert Object Choose File

File **N**ame: | **D**irectories: | OK

c:\notes | Cancel

_backgnd.exe
_bsafe.dll | 📂 c:\
_chronos.exe | 📂 notes
_compute.dll | 📁 data
_computf.dll | 📁 tour
_computn.dll
_dbnotes.dll
_designl.dll

Dri**v**es:

💾 c: stacvol_dsk

6 Select the Path

You select the path by selecting a drive and a directory.

Selecting a Disk Drive

You change the disk drive from the Drive drop down box.

 Click on the drop down box to open it, then click on the drive that you want. If the list is too long to fit in the box, use the scroll bar to move through it.

Press \<Alt\> + \<V\> and then \<↓\> to open the drop down box. Press the drive letter and then \<Enter\>.

Drive Drop Down Box (Example)

💾 c: stacvol_dsk
💾 a:
💾 b:
💾 c: stacvol_dsk
💾 d:

Selecting a Directory

You change the directory from the Directories list box. To reach a sub-directory you must first select its parent directory. To select a directory:

 Double-click on the directory or its folder icon. Use the scroll bars to move up and down the directory tree.

Press \<Alt\> + \<D\> to access the list box, use the cursor keys to highlight the directory, then press \<Enter\>.

Directories List Box (Example)

📂 c:\
📂 notes
📁 data
📁 tour

⑦ Select the File

You select the file from the list section of the File Name combo box. The selected file appears in the combo box's text section.

🖱 Click on the file. If the entire list doesn't fit in the box, use the scroll bars to move through it.

⌨ To access the list section, Press <Alt> + <N>, then press <Tab> once. Press the first character of the file's name until it is highlighted, or highlight it with the cursor keys.

Narrowing the File List

You can narrow the file list by typing characters in the text section of the combo box, and then pressing <Enter>. An asterisk ("*") equals any group of characters, and a question mark ("?") equals any single character. To see only those files with a certain file extension, enter "*" plus the extension. (For example, to see text files, enter "*.TXT".) To access the text section:

🖱 Double-click in it to overwrite the text. Click in it once to edit.

⌨ Press <Alt> + <N>.

⑧ Select the "OK" Button

🖱 Click on it.

⌨ Press <Alt> + <O>.

Notes will embed the file and display it in the selected format. With the picture display format, some applications display their program icon instead of the data. If so, you can try again using another format, or you can open the object in its native application when you want to view it. See "Editing an OLE Object" below.

Editing an OLE Object

You edit an OLE object in its native application. To open the object:

🖱 Double-click on it.

⌨ Use the cursor keys to highlight it, then select "Edit Object" from the Edit menu. Press <Alt> + <E>, then <O>.

To send your work back to Notes, select "Update" from the native application's File menu.

Pop-Ups

Pop-ups provide a little extra information, typically definitions. A pop-up appears as text surrounded by a box. Notes' documentation states that the color of pop-up boxes is green, but some users report the color as brown. When you activate a pop-up, Notes displays a "floating" box that contains text:

Pop-Up (Example)

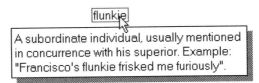

To create a pop-up, follow these steps:

1 Select the "Host" Text

Highlight the text that you want the pop-up to pop from. For help, see "Selecting Text with the Mouse" (page 61) or "Selecting Text with the Keyboard" (page 61).

Bug Alert!

Notes' documentation says that you can use a graphic image as the pop-up host. The author tried it, with little luck: three out of the four times, his computer froze up solid. There may be some connection to the image's size, since the one time that it did work was with a small bitmap.

---

2 Access the "Insert PopUp" Dialog Box

To access the Insert PopUp dialog box, select "PopUp" from the Edit Insert sub-menu.

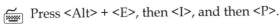 Click on "Edit" in the menu bar, click on "Insert" in the Edit menu, then click on "PopUp" in the sub-menu.

 Press <Alt> + <E>, then <I>, and then <P>.

Click on the Edit Insert Popup[2] SmartIcon.

---

[2] In various places, Notes uses "PopUp", "Popup", "popup", and "pop-up". Don'cha love consistency?

Insert PopUp Dialog Box

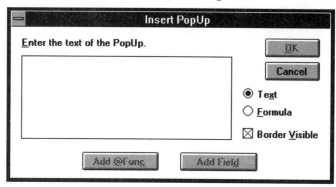

3 Select the "Text" Option

You can create a text pop-up or a formula pop-up. The latter is beyond the scope of this book, so select the Text option now.

🖰 Click on "Text" or the option button.

⌨ Press <Alt> + <X>.

4 Enter the Text

You enter the pop-up's text in the roomy text box. To access the text box:

🖰 Click in it.

⌨ Press <Alt> + <E>.

5 Set the "Borders Visible" Option

If you turn the Borders Visible option on, Notes will display a box around the text that hosts the pop-up. The option is on when the check box is filled and off when the check box is empty. To turn the option on or off:

🖰 Click on "Borders Visible" or the check box.

⌨ Press <Alt> + <V>.

6 Select the "OK" Button

🖰 Click on it.

⌨ Press <Alt> + <O>.

Editing a Pop-Up

To edit a pop-up:

① Put the document in edit mode.

② Double-click on the host text. Notes will open the Insert PopUp dialog box.

③ Make your changes. For more help, start at step 3 on the preceding page.

④ Select the OK button.

Resizing a Picture

Like many computer chores, when you're resizing a picture in Notes, the mouse is quick and dirty, and the keyboard is slow and accurate.

Resizing a Picture with the Mouse

When you select a picture, Notes displays a resizing box at the picture's lower-right corner. You can resize the picture by grabbing the box, dragging it to the appropriate location, and dropping it. In more detail:

① Click once on the picture to select it. Notes displays the resizing box at the picture's lower-right corner.

② Grab the resizing box. Point at it, then press and hold the primary mouse button.

③ Drag the box. Hold the mouse button while you move the mouse. To enlarge the picture, drag the box down or to the right. To reduce the picture, drag the box up or to the left.

④ Drop the box by releasing the mouse button.

Resizing a Picture with the Keyboard

To resize a picture with the keyboard, you select the picture, select "Resize Picture" from the Edit menu, then use the cursor keys to change the picture's size. In more detail:

① Use the cursor keys to select the picture. Notes displays the resizing box at the picture's lower-right corner.

② Select "Resize Picture" from the Edit menu. Press <Alt> + <E>, then <R>. If you have field help turned on, Notes will display "Width/Height = 1.00 / 1.00" in the field help area. (See "Getting Help with Fields" on page 55.)

③ Use the arrow keys to resize the picture. Press <↓> to increase its height and <↑> to reduce it. Press <→> to increase its width and <←> to reduce it.

④ Press <Enter> when you're done.

Special Characters

Notes uses the ANSI[3] character set to display and print characters. You cannot print special characters if your printer does not support the ANSI character set.

Notes uses the Lotus Multibyte Character Set (LMBCS) to store characters. You use *compose sequences* and LMBCS codes to enter special characters. A compose sequence is two characters that represents a special character. The following tables list the special characters that you can use, the compose sequences for those characters that have them, and the LMBCS codes.

Using a Compose Sequence

To use a compose sequence, press <Alt> + <F1>, then type the characters listed in the third column of the following tables. For example, to enter "±", press <Alt> + <F1> and type "+-". Unless otherwise noted, compose sequences aren't sensitive to order, so typing "-+" would yield the same result.

Using an LMBCS Code

To use an LMBCS code:

① Press <Alt> + <F1> twice

② Type "0-"

③ Type the characters listed in the fourth column of the following tables

---

[3] American National Standards Institute

For example, to enter the paragraph symbol ("¶"), press <Alt> + <F1> twice, then type "0-244".

Arithmetic and Geometry

Character	Description	Compose Sequence	Code
x	multiplication	XX *or* xx	158
±	plus / minus	+-	241
÷	division	:-	246
°	degree	^0	248

Currency

Character	Description	Compose Sequence	Code
£	pound (UK)	L= *or* l= *or* L- *or* l-	156
¥	yen (Japan)	Y= *or* y= *or* Y- *or* y-	190
¢	cent (USA, Canada, etc.)	C| *or* c| *or* C/ *or* c/	189

Editing Symbols

Character	Description	Compose Sequence	Code
¶	paragraph symbol		244
§	section symbol		245
|	start of line	-]	170

Fractions

Character	Description	Compose Sequence	Code
½	half	12	171
¼	quarter	14	172
¾	three quarters	34	243

Miscellaneous

Character	Description	Compose Sequence	Code
|	overline	^_	238
¹	1 superscript	^1	251
³	3 superscript	^3	252
²	2 superscript	^2	253
ð	Eth lower	d-	208
Ð	Eth upper	D-	209
°	degree	^0	248
¦	vertical line, broken	/<Spacebar>	221
¤	international currency	XO *or* xo *or* X0 *or* x0	207

Non-English Letters

Character	Description	Compose Sequence	Code
µ	Greek mu, lowercase	/u	230
ß	German sharp, lowercase	ss	225
Æ	AE diphthong	In Order: AE	146
æ	ae diphthong	In Order: ae	145
þ	Icelandic thorn, lowercase	p-	231
Þ	Icelandic thorn, uppercase	P-	232

Punctuation

Character	Description	Compose Sequence	Code
'	close single quote		039
`	open single quote		096
~	tilde	- -	126
¿	inverted question mark	??	168
¡	inverted exclamation mark	!!	173
«	left angle quotes	<<	174
»	right angle quotes	>>	175
-	hyphen	-=	240
¸	cedilla	, ,	247
¨	umlaut		249
·	center dot	^.	250
´	acute		239

Special Symbols

Character	Description	Compose Sequence	Code
@	"at" sign	aa *or* AA	064
ª	feminine ordinal indicator	a_ *or* A_	166
º	masculine ordinal indicator	O_ *or* o_	167
®	registered	RO *or* R0 *or* r0	169
©	copyright	CO *or* co *or* C0 *or* c0	184

Accented Letters

A, a

Character	Description	Compose Sequence	Code
Á	acute	A'	181
á	acute	a'	160
Å	angstrom	A*	143
å	angstrom	a*	134
Â	circumflex	A^	182
â	circumflex	a^	131
À	grave	A`	183
à	grave	a`	133
Ã	tilde	A~	199
ã	tilde	a~	198
Ä	umlaut	A"	142
ä	umlaut	a"	132

C, c

Character	Description	Compose Sequence	Code
Ç	cedilla	C,	128
ç	cedilla	c,	135

E, e

Character	Description	Compose Sequence	Code
É	acute	E'	144
é	acute	e'	130
Ê	circumflex	E^	210
ê	circumflex	e^	136
È	grave	E`	212
è	grave	e'	138
Ë	umlaut	E"	211
ë	umlaut	e"	137

I, i

Character	Description	Compose Sequence	Code
Í	acute	I'	214
í	acute	i'	161
Î	circumflex	I^	215
î	circumflex	i^	140
Ì	grave	I`	222
ì	grave	i`	141
Ï	umlaut	I"	216
ï	umlaut	i"	139

N, n

Character	Description	Compose Sequence	Code
Ñ	tilde	N~	165
ñ	tilde	n~	164

O, o

Character	Description	Compose Sequence	Code
Ó	acute	O'	224
ó	acute	o'	162
Ô	circumflex	O^	226
ô	circumflex	o^	147
Ò	grave	O`	227
ò	grave	o`	149
Ø	slash	O/	157
ø	slash	o/	155
Õ	tilde	O~	229
õ	tilde	o~	228
Ö	umlaut	O"	153
ö	umlaut	o"	148

U, u

Character	Description	Compose Sequence	Code
Ú	acute	U'	233
ú	acute	u'	163
Û	circumflex	U^	234
û	circumflex	u^	150
Ù	grave	U`	235
ù	grave	u`	151
Ü	umlaut	U"	154
ü	umlaut	u"	129

Y, y

Character	Description	Compose Sequence	Code
Ý	acute	Y'	237
ý	acute	y'	236
ÿ	umlaut	y"	152

Creating and Editing Tables

> **Tip:** Notes' tools for creating and editing tables are crude and difficult to work with. You may find it easier to create and edit your tables in another application (such as a word processor or a spreadsheet), then bring them into Notes as OLE objects (see page 74), or by importing them (see "Importing a File" on page 72).
>
> *A word of warning:* depending on the application, you may lose some or all of the table's formatting, especially borders. Trial and error is the only way to determine what works best with the tools at hand.

Creating a Table

You create a table from the Insert Table dialog box. You access the dialog box by selecting "Table" from the Edit Insert sub-menu.

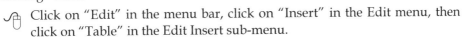 Click on "Edit" in the menu bar, click on "Insert" in the Edit menu, then click on "Table" in the Edit Insert sub-menu.

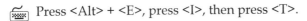 Press <Alt> + <E>, press <I>, then press <T>.

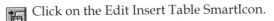 Click on the Edit Insert Table SmartIcon.

Insert Table Dialog Box

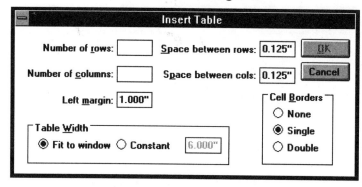

Text Input

You set the following parameters by typing in the appropriate text boxes:

- Number of Rows
- Space Between Rows
- Left Margin
- Number of Columns
- Space Between Columns

To access a text box:

Double-click in it to highlight the current text so that you can overwrite it. Click once to edit the current text.

Press <Alt> plus the text box's underlined letter, or press <Tab> until the text is highlighted.

Table Width

The Fit to Window Option makes the table as wide as the document's text area, and the Constant Option sets the table's width to a specified amount. To select an option:

Click on the label or its option button.

Press <Alt> + <W>, then use the cursor keys to highlight it.

If you select the Constant option, you have to enter the new table's width in the option's text box. Press <Tab> to access the text box (or click in it), then type the amount.

Cell Borders

You select cell borders from the Cell Borders group box.

Click on the type of borders that you want.

Press <Alt> + <B>, then use the cursor keys to highlight the border type.

Adding Rows and Columns

To add rows or columns to a table, follow these steps:

1 | Place the Insertion Point in the Table

You can insert rows or columns into the table, or you can add rows or columns to the end of the table.

Inserting Rows or Columns into the Table

To insert rows or columns into the table, place the insertion point in the row or column that you want to follow the new rows or columns. For example, if you want to add a row at the beginning of the table, place the insertion point in the table's first row.

Adding Rows or Columns to the End of the Table

To add rows or columns to the end of the table, place the insertion point in any row and column.

2 | Access the "Insert Row/Column" Dialog Box

Select "Insert Row/Column" from the Edit Table sub-menu.

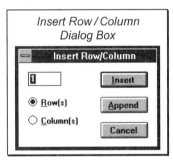

Insert Row/Column Dialog Box

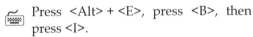 Click on "Edit" in the menu bar, click on "Table" in the Edit menu, then click on "Insert Row/Column" in the sub-menu.

Press <Alt> + <E>, press <B>, then press <I>.

Click on the Edit Table Insert Row/Column SmartIcon.

3 | Enter the Number of Rows or Columns

Type the number into the text box. To access the text box:

Double-click in it.

Press <Tab> until the current number is highlighted.

4 | Select Rows or Columns

Click on "Row(s)" or "Column(s)".

Press <Alt> + <R> for rows, or <Alt> + <C> for columns.

5 | Select the Appropriate Button

The Insert button inserts the rows or columns before the current row or column. The Append button adds the rows or columns to the end of the table. The Cancel button closes the dialog box without doing anything.

🖱 Click on the button.

⌨ Press <Alt> + <I> to insert, <Alt> + <A> to append, and <Esc> to cancel.

Deleting Rows and Columns

To delete rows or columns from a table, follow these steps:

1 | Place the Insertion Point in the Table

Place the insertion point in the first row or column that you want to delete. For example, if you want to delete the second and third columns, place the insertion point in the second column. For help positioning the insertion point, see page 60.

2 | Access the "Delete Row/Column" Dialog Box

Select "Delete Row/Column" from the Edit Table sub-menu.

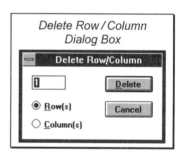

Delete Row/Column
Dialog Box

🖱 Click on "Edit" in the menu bar, click on "Table" in the Edit menu, then click on "Delete Row/Column" in the sub-menu.

⌨ Press <Alt> + <E>, press <B>, then press <D>.

▦ Click on the Edit Table Delete Row Column SmartIcon.

3 | Enter the Number of Rows or Columns

Type the number into the text box. To access the text box:

🖱 Double-click in it.

⌨ Press <Tab> until the current number is highlighted.

4 | Select What You're Deleting — Rows or Columns

🖱 Click on "Row(s)" or "Column(s)".

⌨ Press <Alt> + <R> for rows, or <Alt> + <C> for columns.

5 Select the "Delete" Button

🖱 Click on it.

⌨ Press <Alt> + <D>.

To close the dialog box without deleting rows or columns, click on the Cancel button, or press <Esc>.

6 Respond to the Prompt

If you selected the Delete button on the previous step, Notes will present the following prompt:

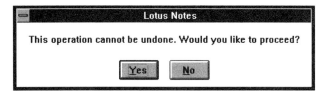

▶ Click on the Yes button (or press <Alt> + <Y>) to delete the selected rows or columns.

▶ Click on the No button (or press <Alt> + <N>) to cancel the deletion and return to the Delete Row/Column dialog box.

Deleting a Table

There are two ways to delete a table:

▶ You can use the Delete Row / Column Function to delete all of its rows or columns. See "Deleting Rows and Columns" on the preceding page.

▶ You can select it (see page 97) and delete it like normal text.

The second method is not only easier, it's also undo-able (see "Edit Undo" on page 62). The first method is permanent.

Formatting Tables

You format a table from the Edit Table Format dialog box. (For help formatting a table's text, see "Applying Text and Paragraph Formats" on page 97.) You access the dialog box by selecting "Format" from the Edit Table sub-menu.

Click on "Edit" in the menu bar, click on "Table" in the Edit menu, then click on "Format" in the Edit Table sub-menu.

Press <Alt> + <E>, press <B>, then press <F>.

Click on the Edit Table Format SmartIcon.

Edit Table Format Dialog Box

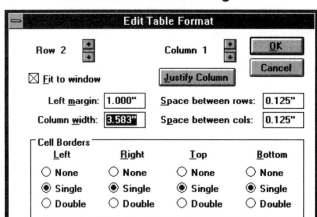

Global Settings

The global settings affect the entire table:

- Fit to Window Option
- Left Margin
- Space Between Rows
- Space Between Columns

Edit Table Format Dialog Box: Global Settings (Example)

```
┌──────────────────────────────────────────────────┐
│                  Edit Table Format                 │
│                                                    │
│   Row 2  [▲▼]        Column 1  [▲▼]   ┌─── OK ───┐ │
│                                        └──────────┘ │
│   ⊠ Fit to window      │ Justify Column │  Cancel   │
│                                                    │
│      Left margin: │1.000"│  Space between rows: │0.125"│ │
│    Column width:  │3.583"│  Space between cols: │0.125"│ │
│   ┌Cell Borders──────────────────────────────────┐ │
│   │  Left        Right       Top      Bottom      │ │
│   │ ○ None      ○ None     ○ None     ○ None       │ │
│   │ ◉ Single    ◉ Single   ◉ Single   ◉ Single     │ │
│   │ ○ Double    ○ Double   ○ Double   ○ Double     │ │
│   └──────────────────────────────────────────────┘ │
└──────────────────────────────────────────────────┘
```

Fit to Window Option

The Fit to Window Option makes the table as wide as the document's text area. Notes maintains the proportion of each column's width to the width of the entire table. The option is on when its check box is filled. To turn the option on or off:

🖱 Click on its label or on the check box.

⌨ Press <Alt> + <F>.

Left Margin and Spacing

You set the table's indent (left margin) and either of the spacing options by accessing the text box and entering the new amount. To access the text boxes:

🖱 Double-click to highlight the text and overwrite it. Click once to edit the current text.

⌨ Press <Alt> plus the setting's underlined letter.

Selecting a Column or Row

You select a column or row using the row and column controls at the top of the Edit Table Format dialog box.

Edit Table Format Dialog Box: Row and Column Controls

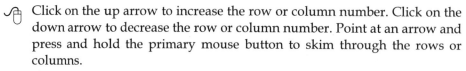 Click on the up arrow to increase the row or column number. Click on the down arrow to decrease the row or column number. Point at an arrow and press and hold the primary mouse button to skim through the rows or columns.

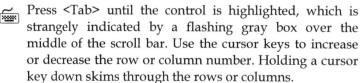 Press <Tab> until the control is highlighted, which is strangely indicated by a flashing gray box over the middle of the scroll bar. Use the cursor keys to increase or decrease the row or column number. Holding a cursor key down skims through the rows or columns.

Highlighted Row Control

Row 1

Column Settings

Column settings affect the current column only. For help selecting a column, see the preceding page.

Column Width

You set the width of the current column by accessing the Column Width text box and entering the new amount. To access the text box:

 Double-click to highlight the text and overwrite it. Click once to edit the current text.

Press <Alt> + <W>.

Justification (Text Alignment)

You set the text alignment for the current column from the Justify Table Column dialog box.

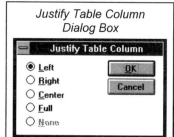 Click on the Justify Column button to access the dialog box. Click on a setting, then click on the OK button. To close the dialog box without changing the justification, click on the Cancel button.

Press <Alt> + <J> to access the dialog box. Press <Alt> plus the setting's underlined letter, then press <Alt> + <O>. To close the dialog box without changing the justification, press <Esc>

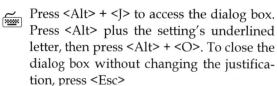

Justify Table Column Dialog Box

Justify Table Column

- ◉ Left
- ○ Right
- ○ Center
- ○ Full
- ○ None

OK

Cancel

Cell Borders

You select cell borders from the Cell Borders group box. Cell border settings affect the current cell only. You select a cell by selecting its column and row (see page 95).

Cell Borders Group Box (Example)

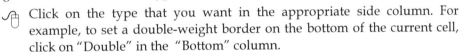

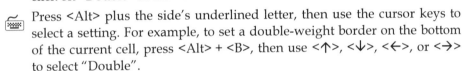

You set a cell's borders by selecting a border type for each of its four sides. A double border is twice as thick as a single border, not two lines placed close together. To select a border type:

Click on the type that you want in the appropriate side column. For example, to set a double-weight border on the bottom of the current cell, click on "Double" in the "Bottom" column.

Press <Alt> plus the side's underlined letter, then use the cursor keys to select a setting. For example, to set a double-weight border on the bottom of the current cell, press <Alt> + <B>, then use <↑>, <↓>, <←>, or <→> to select "Double".

Selecting a Table

You can do two things with a selected table: apply text and paragraph formats (see below), or delete it (see page 93). To select a table:

① Put an empty paragraph before the table and an empty paragraph after it.

② Place the insertion point in the empty paragraph before the table.

③ Use the mouse to drag the insertion point down into the table, or press <Shift> + <↓>.

Applying Text and Paragraph Formats

You can use Notes' features for formatting text and paragraphs to format the contents of a table, but you can only work on the entire table at once — you can't apply formatting to only part of it. For help selecting a table, see above. For help with text and paragraph formatting, see "Formatting Rich Text" on page 99.

Formatting Rich Text

Rich text fields accept text formatting (fonts), paragraph formatting, special characters, tables, OLE objects, and Notes' special document features (doclinks, pop-ups, buttons, and attachments). This chapter covers:

- Applying Fonts (see below)
- Formatting Paragraphs (see page 105)
- Paragraph Styles (see page 112)

Applying Fonts

> **Please Note:** Notes (and many other software products) uses "font" to mean both a typeface alone *and* the entire set of formatting properties applied to a given piece of text (typeface, point size, bold, italic, etc.). Many people (the author included) find this approach confusing. This book uses "font" to mean only the latter: the entire set of properties applied to a given piece of text. A typeface alone is always referred to as a typeface.

Rich text has ten font properties. The *variable properties* — typeface, point size, and color — have a range of settings. For example, Notes offers fifteen different text colors. The *on/off properties* — normal, bold, italic, strikethrough, superscript, and subscript — have only two settings, on and off. Turning the Normal Property on deactivates the other six on/off properties.

When you select font properties, Notes applies the font to any selected text. If no text is selected, it applies the properties to the insertion point, and any text that you enter will have the new formatting. For help, see "Selecting Text with the Mouse"

Font Properties		
Property	**Variable**	**On/Off**
Typeface	✓	
Point Size	✓	
Color	✓	
Normal		✓
Bold		✓
Italic		✓
Underline		✓
Strikethrough		✓
Superscript		✓
Subscript		✓

(page 61) or "Selecting Text with the Keyboard" (page 61). The following table lists the font formatting properties, the features you can use to set them, and where to turn for further help.

Setting Font Properties					
Property	Font Dialog Box	Text Menu	Keyboard	SmartIcon	Status Bar
Typeface	✓				✓
Point Size	✓	✓	✓	✓	✓
Color	✓				
Normal	✓	✓	✓	✓	
Bold	✓	✓	✓	✓	
Italic	✓	✓	✓	✓	
Underline	✓	✓	✓	✓	
Strikethrough	✓				
Superscript	✓				
Subscript	✓				
See	below	page 102	page 102	page 102	page 104

Font Dialog Box

To access the Font dialog box when you're editing text:

Select "Font" from the Text menu. Click on "Text" in the menu bar, then click on "Font".

Press <Ctrl> + <K>.

Click on the Text Font SmartIcon.

You can also access the Font dialog box by selecting the Fonts button on the Edit Header/Footer Dialog Box (see page 63).

Font Dialog Box

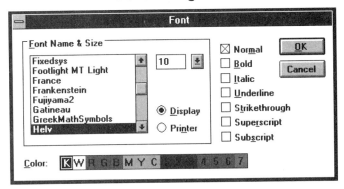

Selecting a Typeface

You select a typeface from the Font Name list box. Some typefaces are designed strictly for computer display, while others are designed to be displayed and printed.

Font Name List Box

Fixedsys
Footlight MT Light
France
Frankenstein
Fujiyama2
Gatineau
GreekMathSymbols
Helv

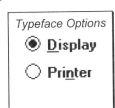

Typeface Options

▶ To list all typefaces, turn the Display option on. Click on "Display" or its option button, or press <Alt> + <D>.

▶ To list only printable typefaces, turn the Printer option on. Click on "Printer" or its option button, or press <Alt> + <N>.

To select a typeface:

 Click on it. Use the scroll bar to move through the list.

Press <Alt> + <F> to access the list. Use the cursor keys to highlight the typeface.

Selecting a Point Size

You select a point size from the Point Size combo box. To select a point size:

Point Size Combo Box

Click on the down arrow to open the combo box, then click on the point size that you want to select.

Press <Tab> until the text in the combo box is highlighted, then type that point size that you want to use, or use the cursor keys to move through the list.

Selecting a Color

You select a color from the Color display box. To select a color:

Color Display Box

 Click on it.

Press <Alt> + <C> to access the display box, then press the color's letter or number, or use the cursor keys to highlight it.

Setting an On / Off Property

You turn an on/off property on by filling in its check box. Turning the Normal Property on automatically deactivates all the other on/off properties. To change an on/off setting:

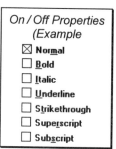

On / Off Properties
(Example
☒ Normal
☐ Bold
☐ Italic
☐ Underline
☐ Strikethrough
☐ Superscript
☐ Subscript

Click on the check box or its label.

Press <Alt> plus the property's underlined letter. For example, to turn bold on or off, press <Alt> + <B>.

Closing the Font Dialog Box

▶ To close the Font dialog box and apply the selected formatting properties, click on the OK button, or press <Alt> + <O>.

▶ To close the Font dialog box and cancel the selected formatting properties, click on the Cancel button, or press <Esc>.

Text Menu, Keyboard, and SmartIcons

The following table outlines the Text menu selections, keyboard commands, and SmartIcons for formatting text. The last two commands, Enlarge Point Size and Reduce Point Size, raise and lower the point size by one selection respectively. For example, if the current setting is ten points and the next is twelve, pressing <F2> will change the point size from ten points to twelve.

Formatting Text: Text Menu, Keyboard, and SmartIcons				
Property or Command	**On/Off**	**Text Menu Selection**	**Keys**	**SmartIcon**
Normal	✓	"Normal"	<Ctrl> + <T>	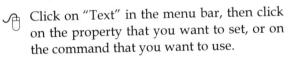
Bold	✓	"Bold"	<Ctrl> + <B>	
Italic	✓	"Italic"	<Ctrl> + <I>	
Underline	✓	"Underline"	<Ctrl> + <U>	
Enlarge Point Size		"Enlarge"	<F2>	
Reduce Point Size		"Reduce"	<Shift> + <F2>	

Tip: If you forget the hot keys for a formatting property, they're listed on the Text menu (see diagram below).

Using the Text Menu

When an on/off property is set to on, a check appears next to it on the Text menu. To set a formatting property from the Text menu:

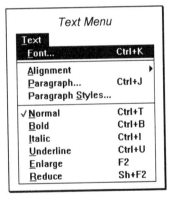

Text Menu

Click on "Text" in the menu bar, then click on the property that you want to set, or on the command that you want to use.

Press <Alt> + <T>, then press the property or command's underlined letter.

Status Bar

You can set the typeface and the point size from the Status Bar.

Typeface Indicator

The Typeface Indicator displays the typeface at the insertion point. The indicator is active when you're in Edit Mode, and blank when you're not. Clicking on the indicator opens a typeface pop-up menu. To choose a typeface:

 Click on it.

 Use the cursor keys to highlight it and press <Enter>. You can move through the list by pressing character keys. For example, pressing <F> will take you to the first typeface that begins with "F", and pressing <F> again will take you to the second typeface that begins with "F".

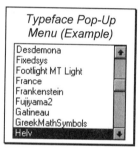

Point Size Indicator

The Point Size Indicator displays the text size at the insertion point. The indicator is active when you're in Edit Mode, and blank when you're not. Clicking on the indicator opens a point size pop-up menu. To choose a point size:

 Click on it.

 Use the cursor keys to highlight it and press <Enter>. You can move through the list by pressing number keys. For example, pressing <2> will take you to the first point size that begins with "2", and pressing <2> again will take you to the second point size that begins with "2".

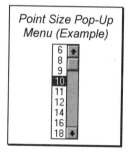

Formatting Paragraphs

> **Important!** When you set paragraph properties, Notes applies the properties to any selected text. If no text is selected, it applies the properties to the paragraph that currently contains the insertion point. For help, see "Selecting Text with the Mouse" (page 61) or "Selecting Text with the Keyboard" (page 61).

Paragraphs have six groups of formatting properties. The following table lists the six groups, the features you can use to set them, and where to turn for further help.

Setting Paragraph Properties					
Properties Group	**Text Paragraph Dialog Box**	**Menus**	**SmartIcons**	**Ruler**	**Paragraph Styles**
Margins	✓		✓	✓	✓
Pagination	✓	✓	✓		✓
Tabs	✓			✓	✓
Hide	✓				✓
Alignment	✓	✓	✓		✓
Spacing	✓				✓
See	following page	page 109	page 109	page 111	page 112

"Show Page Breaks" Option

To get a better idea how your document will print out, turn the Show Page Breaks option on. The option is on when a check mark appears next to it on the View menu. To turn the Show Page Breaks option on or off:

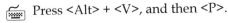 Click on "View" in the menu bar, then click on "Show Page Breaks".

Press <Alt> + <V>, and then <P>.

"Text Paragraph" Dialog Box

You can set all of the paragraph properties from the Text Paragraph dialog box. To access the dialog box:

🖱 Select "Paragraph" from the Text menu. Click on "Text" in the menu bar, then click on "Paragraph".

⌨ Press <Ctrl> + <J>.

▦ Click on the Text Paragraph SmartIcon.

You can also access the Text Paragraph dialog box by selecting the Paragraph button in the Text Paragraph Styles dialog box. See "Creating a Style" on page 114 or see "Editing a Style" on page 115.

Text Paragraph Dialog Box

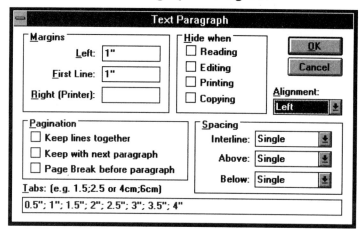

Margins

The margins determine where the paragraphs will appear horizontally relative to the page. You set the margins from the Margin group box. The Right Margin only affects the display on your computer screen if the Show Page Breaks option is on (see the preceding page). To set a margin, access its text box, then type the new margin. To access a margin text box:

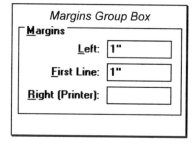

Margins Group Box

🖱 Double-click in it if you want to highlight the text and overwrite it. Click in it once if you want to edit the current text.

⌨ Press <Alt> plus the underlined letter, or press <Tab> until the text is highlighted.

Pagination Options

The pagination options affect where the page breaks will fall when the paragraphs are printed. When you're changing paragraph pagination, it can be helpful to turn the Show Page Breaks option on (see page 105).

Option:	Effect:
Keep Lines Together	Notes attempts to print the entire paragraph on a single page. Notes breaks the paragraph only if it won't fit on a single page.
Keep with Next Paragraph	Notes prints the paragraph on the same page as the following paragraph.
Page Break Before Paragraph	Notes inserts a page break before the paragraph, so that it appears at the top of a new page.

You set the pagination options from the Pagination group box. To turn an option on or off:

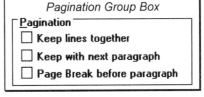

🖱 Click on the option's label or check box.

⌨ Press <Alt> + <P>, use the cursor keys to highlight the option, and press <Spacebar>.

Tabs

Creating tab stops from the Text Paragraph dialog box is a rather crude process: you type the whole lump of them into the Tabs text box, separating the individual stops with semicolons ("`;`").

> *Tabs Text Box (Example)*
> T̲abs: (e.g. 1.5;2.5 or 4cm;6cm)
> 0.5"; 1"; 1.5"; 2"; 2.5"; 3"; 3.5"; 4"

Contrary to Notes' own directions, you can ignore the units, which can be inches or centimeters, because it's handled automatically. Use decimals for non-integer settings; for example, type 1.5 instead of 1½. To access the Tabs text box:

🖱 Double-click on a tab stop to highlight it and its semicolon. Click once to access the text box without highlighting any text.

⌨ Press <Alt> + <T>. Notes will highlight the entire contents of the text box. You can also press <Tab> until the text is highlighted.

> **Tip:** Unless you hate using the mouse, you'll find it easier to create tabs from the Ruler (see page 111).

Hide Options

The hide options control the display and printing of the selected paragraphs.

Option:	Effect:
Reading	Selected paragraphs are not displayed when the document is viewed on-screen, and are omitted when the document is printed out.
Editing	Selected paragraphs are not displayed when the document is being edited.
Printing	Selected paragraphs are omitted when the document is printed out.
Copying	Selected paragraphs will not copy to the Clipboard when the document is being viewed. Paragraphs will copy when the document is being edited.

You set the hide options from the Hide group box. To turn an option on or off:

 Click on the option's label or check box.

 Press <Alt> + <H>, use the cursor keys to highlight the option, and press <Spacebar>.

Hide Group Box

Alignment

The alignment property controls the horizontal placement of the selected paragraphs.

Setting:	Description:
Left	Align text flush with left margin
Right	Align text flush with right margin
Center	Center text between margins
Full	Justify text to meet margins
None	Place entire paragraph on a single line

You set the alignment property from the Alignment drop down box.

 Click on the drop down box to open it, then click on the setting that you want to select.

 Press <Alt> + <A> to access the drop down box. Press the first letter of the setting that you want to select, or use the cursor keys to move through the list.

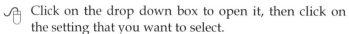

Alignment Drop Down Box

Spacing

The spacing properties control the vertical distance between paragraphs and between lines of text.

Property:	Description:
Interline	Amount of space between lines of text within a paragraph
Above	Amount of space between current paragraph and preceding paragraph
Below	Amount of space between current paragraph and subsequent paragraph

Note that the Below property of one paragraph and the Above property of the next paragraph combine to determine how far apart the two paragraphs will be (see diagram at right).

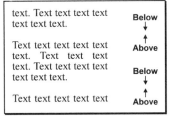

You set a spacing property from its drop down box in the Spacing group box. To set a property:

 Click on the drop down box to open it, then click on the setting that you want to select.

Press <Alt> + <S> to access the Interline drop down box, then (if necessary) press <Tab> to reach the drop down box that you want. Press the first letter of the setting that you want to select, or use the cursor keys to move through the list.

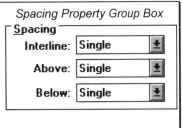

Spacing Property Group Box

Spacing
Interline: Single
Above: Single
Below: Single

Menus, Keyboard, and SmartIcons

The following table outlines the menu selections, keyboard commands, and SmartIcons for formatting paragraphs. The final column indicates how the command can be undone. A check mark ("✓") indicates that the command can be reversed with the standard Edit Undo command (see page 62). Most of the menu commands appear on the Text Alignment sub-menu and the Edit Insert sub-menu. To make a menu selection using the table:

① Click on selection 1 in the menu bar.

② Click on selection 2 in the menu.

③ If there is a selection 3, click on it in the sub-menu.

Press the keys in the order listed.

Formatting Paragraphs: Menus, Keyboard, and SmartIcons					
Command	Description	Menu Selections	Keys	SmartIcon	Undo
Align Left	Aligns text flush with left margin	① "Text" ② "Alignment" ③ "Left"	① \<Alt\> + \<T\> ② \<A\> ③ \<L\>		✓
Align Right	Aligns text flush with right margin	① "Text" ② "Alignment" ③ "Right"	① \<Alt\> + \<T\> ② \<A\> ③ \<R\>		✓
Align Center	Centers text between margins	① "Text" ② "Alignment" ③ "Center"	① \<Alt\> + \<T\> ② \<A\> ③ \<C\>		✓
Align Full	Justifies text to meet margins	① "Text" ② "Alignment" ③ "Full"	① \<Alt\> + \<T\> ② \<A\> ③ \<F\>		✓
Align None	Places entire paragraph on a single line	① "Text" ② "Alignment" ③ "None"	① \<Alt\> + \<T\> ② \<A\> ③ \<N\>	-None-	✓
Indent	Incrementally indents paragraph	-None-	\<F8\>		\<Shift\> + \<F8\>
Indent First Line	Incrementally indents first line	-None-	\<F7\>		\<Shift\> + \<F7\>
Page Break	Adds/removes page break before	① "Edit" ② "Insert" ③ "Page Break"	\<Ctrl\> + \<L\>		✓
Show Ruler	Displays/hides the Ruler (see following page)	① "View" ② "Show Ruler"	\<Ctrl\> + \<R\>		✓

The Ruler

Please Note: You use the Ruler with the mouse. You <u>cannot</u> use the Ruler with the keyboard. If you do not have a mouse, or hate using it, don't bother reading this section.

You can use the Ruler to set margins and tabs. When you turn the Show Ruler option on, Notes displays the Ruler at the top of the document window.

The Ruler (Example)

Showing and Hiding the Ruler

To turn the Show Ruler option on or off:

Select "Show Ruler" from the View menu. Click on "View" in the menu bar, then click on "Show Ruler".

Press <Ctrl> + <R>.

Click on the View Show Ruler SmartIcon.

Ruler Symbols

There are five ruler symbols for margins and tabs:

Ruler Symbols: Margins and Tabs	
Symbol	**Description**
	First line indent
▼	Left margin
▶	First line indent and left margin coincide. Combination of two previous symbols.
↑	Tab stop
◀	Right margin. Only visible when "Show Page Breaks" Option is on (see page 105).

Adjusting a Setting's Position

To move an indent, tab stop, or margin, you *grab* the appropriate symbol, *drag* it to the new location, and *drop* it. You grab a symbol by pointing at it, then pressing and holding the primary mouse button. You drag a symbol by moving the mouse. You drop a symbol by releasing the mouse button. For example:

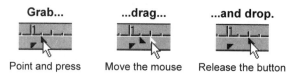

Grab...	...drag...	...and drop.
Point and press	Move the mouse	Release the button

When Left Margin and Indent Coincide

Changing the left margin or first line indent can get a little tricky if the two happen to coincide. To change the indent, you grab the top half of the bigger, combined wedge. To change the margin, you grab the bottom half.

Combined Wedge
First Indent
Left Margin

When you drag the appropriate half, the other half will stay behind, and you'll wind up with two separate symbols.

Adding and Removing Tab Stops

To add a new tab stop, click on the Ruler where you want the stop to be. To remove a tab stop, click on its symbol.

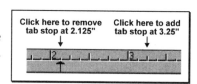

Click here to remove tab stop at 2.125"

Click here to add tab stop at 3.25"

Paragraph Styles

A paragraph style is a named set of paragraph properties. Styles do not include text formatting properties (typeface, color, etc.). You use styles to keep your paragraph formatting consistent, and to quickly apply sets of properties.

Accessing the "Text Paragraph Styles" Dialog Box

You create and apply styles from the Text Paragraph Styles dialog box. To access the dialog box, select "Paragraph Styles" from the Text menu.

Click on "Text" in the menu bar, then click on "Paragraph Styles".

 Press <Alt> + <T>, then press <S>.

Text Paragraph Styles Dialog Box (Example)

```
┌──────────────────────────────────────────────┐
│ ─        Text Paragraph Styles               │
├──────────────────────────────────────────────┤
│  Style Name                                    │
│  ┌────────────────┐ ┌─────────┐ ┌─────────┐    │
│  │[None]        ▲ │ │  Apply  │ │  Done   │    │
│  │ Bullets        │ └─────────┘ └─────────┘    │
│  │ Defined Term   │ ┌─────────┐ ┌─────────┐    │
│  │ Heading 1      │ │  New    │ │ Delete  │    │
│  │ Heading 2      │ └─────────┘ └─────────┘    │
│  │ Normal       ▼ │   ┌────────────────┐       │
│  └────────────────┘   │   Paragraph... │       │
│                       └────────────────┘       │
│      New Style Name: ┌────────────────────────┐│
│                      └────────────────────────┘│
└──────────────────────────────────────────────┘
```

Applying a Style / Removing Styles

To apply a style, or to remove a style or styles, follow these steps:

1 Select the Paragraphs

Highlight the paragraphs that you want to change. The selection can begin anywhere in the first paragraph and end anywhere in the second paragraph. For a single paragraph, just placing the insertion point in it will suffice. For help, see "Selecting Text with the Mouse" (page 61) or "Selecting Text with the Keyboard" (page 61).

2 Access the "Text Paragraph Styles" Dialog Box

Select "Paragraph Styles" from the Text menu.

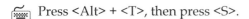 Click on "Text" in the menu bar, then click on "Paragraph Styles".

Press <Alt> + <T>, then press <S>.

The styles of the paragraphs you selected determine which entry is highlighted in the Style Name list box.

- If the paragraphs don't have any styles, the "(None)" selection is highlighted.

- If the paragraphs only have one style, that style is highlighted.

- If the paragraphs have more than one style, none of the entries are highlighted.

3 Select the Style, or Select "(None)"

You select a style from the Style Name list box. If you want to remove the styles from the selected paragraphs, choose "(None)".

🖱 Click on the style that you want. If the list is too long to fit in the box, you can use the scroll bar to move through it.

⌨ Press <Alt> + <S> to access the list box. You can use the cursor keys to move through the list, or you can press the first letter of the style name until the correct style is highlighted. For example, to select "Heading 2" in the diagram on the preceding page, you would press <H> twice.

4 Select the "Apply" Button

🖱 Click on it.

⌨ Press <Alt> + <A>.

Notes will close the dialog box and apply the style selection. To close the dialog box without applying the style selection, select the Done button.

Creating a Style

To create a new style, follow these steps:

1 Select a Paragraph to Base the Style On (Optional)

The new style will start with the paragraph properties of the current text selection. Select a paragraph that you want to use as the basis for the new style. For help, see "Selecting Text with the Mouse" (page 61) or "Selecting Text with the Keyboard" (page 61).

2 Access the "Text Paragraph Styles" Dialog Box

Select "Paragraph Styles" from the Text menu.

🖱 Click on "Text" in the menu bar, then click on "Paragraph Styles".

⌨ Press <Alt> + <T>, then press <S>.

3 Enter a Name in the "New Style" Text Box

To access the New Style Name text box, click in it, or press <Alt> + <E>. Type the new style's name.

4 Edit the Format (Optional)

If you're basing the style on an existing paragraph, you probably won't need to edit the format. If you do need to edit it, click on the Paragraph button, or press <Alt> + <P>. Notes will open the Text Paragraph dialog box. For more help, see page 106.

5 Select the "New" Button

Selecting the New button adds the style to the document and to the Style Name list box.

Click on the button.

Press <Alt> + <N>.

6 Apply the Style (Optional)

If you want to change the current paragraph to the new style, select the Apply button. You'll probably want to do this if you used the paragraph as the basis for the style (see step 1).

Click on the button.

Press <Alt> + <A>.

7 Select the "Done" Button

Click on it.

Press <Alt> + <O>.

Notes will close the Text Paragraph Styles dialog box.

Editing a Style

To edit a style, follow these steps:

1 Access the "Text Paragraph Styles" Dialog Box

Select "Paragraph Styles" from the Text menu.

Click on "Text" in the menu bar, then click on "Paragraph Styles".

Press <Alt> + <T>, then press <S>.

2   Select the Style

You select a style from the Style Name list box.

Click on the style that you want. If the list is too long to fit in the box, you can use the scroll bar to move through it.

Press <Alt> + <S> to access the list box. You can use the cursor keys to move through the list, or you can press the first letter of the style name until the correct style is highlighted. For example, to select "Heading 2" in the diagram on page 113, you would press <H> twice.

3   Edit the Format

Click on the Paragraph button, or press <Alt> + <P>. Notes will open the Text Paragraph dialog box. For more help, see page 106.

4   Select the "Done" Button

Click on it.

Press <Alt> + <O>.

Notes will close the Text Paragraph Styles dialog box.

Deleting a Style

When you delete a style, paragraphs that had the deleted style retain the formatting of the deleted style. They do not revert to their previous formats, or automatically change to some other style. To delete a style, follow these steps:

1   Access the "Text Paragraph Styles" Dialog Box

Select "Paragraph Styles" from the Text menu.

Click on "Text" in the menu bar, then click on "Paragraph Styles".

Press <Alt> + <T>, then press <S>.

2 Select the Style

You select a style from the Style Name list box.

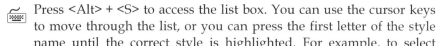

Click on the style that you want. If the list is too long to fit in the box, you can use the scroll bar to move through it.

Press <Alt> + <S> to access the list box. You can use the cursor keys to move through the list, or you can press the first letter of the style name until the correct style is highlighted. For example, to select "Heading 2" in the diagram on page 113, you would press <H> twice.

3 Select the "Delete" Button

Click on it.

Press <Alt> + <D>.

Notes will ask if you're sure about this:

Style Delete Prompt (Example)

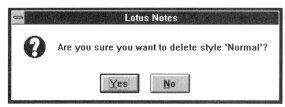

▶ To <u>delete</u> the style, click on the Yes button, or press <Alt> + <Y>. Notes will remove the style from both the Style Name list box and the document.

▶ To <u>save</u> the style, click on the No button, or press <Alt> + <N>.

4 Select the "Done" Button

Click on it.

Press <Alt> + <O>.

Notes will close the Text Paragraph Styles dialog box.

CHAPTER 9

Managing Documents

This chapter covers:

- Selecting Documents (see below)
- Marking Documents as Read or Unread (see page 122)
- Categorizing Documents (see page 124)
- Moving and Copying Documents (see page 126)
- Deleting Documents (see page 126)
- Printing Views and Documents (see page 128)

Selecting Documents

A selected document has a check mark next to it in the marker bar.

Selected Document (Example)

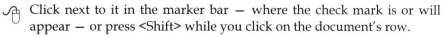

	Holidays	01/21/93	Henri Paquard
✔	Sick Days	01/21/93	Gary Berkowitz
	Company-sponsored Sports Activities	01/21/93	Jose Guarenza

Selecting/Deselecting a Single Document

To select or deselect a single document:

Click next to it in the marker bar — where the check mark is or will appear — or press <Shift> while you click on the document's row.

Use the cursor keys to highlight it, then press <Spacebar>.

Selecting/Deselecting Adjacent Documents

To select or deselect an adjacent group of documents:

Place the cursor next to the first document and over the marker bar. Press and hold the primary mouse button. Drag the cursor down to the last document, then release the mouse button.

Place the cursor anywhere over the first document's row. Press and hold the <Shift> key, then press and hold the primary mouse button. Drag the cursor down to the last document, then release the <Shift> key and the mouse button.

Use the cursor keys to highlight the first document. Press and hold the <Shift> key. Use the cursor keys to highlight the last document, then release the <Shift> key.

Selecting All of the Documents

To select all of the documents:

Select "Select All" from the Edit menu. Click on "Edit" in the menu bar, then click on "Select All".

Press <Ctrl> + <A>.

Click on the Select All SmartIcon.

Deselecting All of the Documents

To deselect all of the documents, select "Deselect All" from the Edit menu.

Click on "Edit" in the menu bar, then click on "Deselect All".

Press <Alt> + <E>, then press <D>.

Selecting Documents by Date

To select documents by date, follow these steps:

1 Access the "Select by Date" Dialog Box

Select "Select by Date" from the Edit menu.

Click on "Edit" in the menu bar, then click on "Select by Date".

Press <Alt> + <E>, then press <B>.

Select by Date Dialog Box

```
┌──────────────────────────────────────────────────┐
│ ─             Select by Date                      │
│                                                    │
│  From:  ┌─────────────────────┐    ┌──────────┐   │
│         │                     │    │    OK    │   │
│         └─────────────────────┘    └──────────┘   │
│  To:    ┌─────────────────────┐    ┌──────────┐   │
│         │                     │    │  Cancel  │   │
│         └─────────────────────┘    └──────────┘   │
│                                                    │
│         ◉ Created                                  │
│         ○ Modified                                 │
│                                                    │
└──────────────────────────────────────────────────┘
```

2 Enter the Dates

You enter a starting date ("From") and an ending date ("To") in the appropriate text boxes, using the "Month/Day/Year" format. To access a text box:

🖰 Double-click in it to highlight the current text for overwriting. Click once to edit the current text.

⌨ Press <Alt> + <F> to access the From text box. Press <Alt> + <T> to access the To text box.

3 Select "Created" or "Modified"

The Created option and the Modified option determine if the date range is for the date the documents were created, or for the last time that they were modified. To select an option:

🖰 Click on it.

⌨ Press <Alt> + <C> for the Created option, and <Alt> + <M> for the Modified option.

4 Select the "OK" Button

🖰 Click on it.

⌨ Press <Alt> + <O>.

Notes will close the Select by Date dialog box and select the appropriate documents. To close the Select by Date dialog box without selecting any documents, click on the Cancel button, or press <Esc>.

Marking Documents Read or Unread

Notes keeps track of which documents you have opened and which you haven't. Documents you have opened are deemed "read" and documents you haven't are deemed "unread". Depending on the database's design, unread documents may be:

- Flagged with an unread marker   ★   Broadcast Rights Revisted
- Flagged and displayed in a different color ★   Broadcast Rights Revisted
- Neither   Broadcast Rights Revisted

This last choice of formatting can be infuriating, although there are situations where it makes some sense — on-line libraries, for example, and Notes' on-line help. Fortunately, you can display only the documents you haven't read (see below), and you can also change a document's status (see below).

Displaying Only Unread Documents

Notes has an easy way to view only the documents that you haven't read: select "Show Only Unread" from the View menu.

🖱 Click on "View" in the Menu Bar, then click on "Show Only Unread".

⌨ Press <Alt> + <V>, then press <U>.

The selections for expanding and contracting the view interact in some unpredictable ways. For more help, see "Expanding and Contracting the View" on page 40.

Setting Documents' Read / Unread Status

You can designate documents as read or unread from the Tools Unread Marks sub-menu or by using SmartIcons.

Using the "Tools Unread Marks" Sub-Menu

To designate documents as read or unread, follow these steps:

1 Select the Documents

If you want to set the status for less than all of the documents, select the appropriate documents now. For help selecting documents, see page 119.

2 Select "Unread Marks" from the "Tools" Menu

🖱️ Click on "Tools" in the menu bar, then click on "Unread Marks".

⌨️ Press <Alt> + <O>, then <M>.

Notes will open the Unread Marks sub-menu.

3 Choose the Status Change

🖱️ Click on it in the sub-menu.

⌨️ Press the underlined letter, or use the cursor keys to highlight it and press <Enter>.

If you're not certain what a selection will do, use the cursor keys to highlight it. Notes will display an explanation of the selection in the main window's title bar.

Using SmartIcons

The following table outlines the SmartIcons that you can use to designate documents as read or unread.

Read / Unread SmartIcons	
SmartIcon	**Description**
	Tools Mark All Read Marks all documents in the active view or selected databases as "read"
	Tools Mark All Unread Marks all documents in the active view or selected databases as "unread"
	Tools Mark Selected Read Marks selected documents in the active view as "read"
	Tools Mark Selected Unread Marks selected documents in the active view as "unread"

Categorizing Documents

Please Note: You cannot categorize documents written by someone else unless your access level for the database is at least Editor. For more information, see "Access Control Lists" on page 34.

To assign documents to a category or categories, follow these steps:

1 Select the Documents

You can categorize documents from a view, and you can categorize the active document. For help selecting documents, see page 119.

2 Access the "Categorize" Dialog Box

Select "Categorize" from the Tools menu.

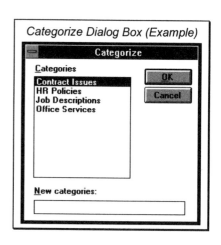

Categorize Dialog Box (Example)

Click on "Tools" in the menu bar, then click on "Categorize".

Press <Alt> + <O>, then <C>.

Click on the Tool Categorize SmartIcon.

3 Select the Categories

Select the categories that you want to add the documents to, and deselect the categories that you want to remove the documents from. If you deselect all of the categories, and don't add a new category (see below), Notes will put the documents under "(Not Categorized)". To select or deselect a category:

Click on it.

Press <Alt> + <C> to access the list box. Use the cursor keys to highlight it (or press its first character until it's highlighted), then press <Spacebar>.

Adding a New Category

To add a new category, enter its name in the New Categories text box. To create multiple categories, separate them with commas. For example, entering "Dairy Products, Vegetables" creates two new categories.

Adding a Sub-Category

To create a sub-category, enter the main category, a backslash, and the new sub-category. For example, entering "Vegetables\Green & Leafy" creates a Green & Leafy sub-category under the Vegetables category. The maximum number of category levels is thirty-two.

Using an Existing Sub-Category

Sub-categories do <u>not</u> appear in the Categorize dialog box. To use an existing subcategory, type its full name (such as "Vegetables\Green & Leafy") into the New Categories text box. If you can't see a certain sub-category in the view, make sure that the category level above it is expanded.

4 | Select the "OK" Button

 Click on it.

Press <Alt> + <O>.

Notes will reassign the selected documents.

Deleting a Category

You delete a category by removing all of its documents. There are three ways to remove documents from a category:

▶ Delete them from the database (the drastic approach).

▶ Assign them to a different category or categories. If they're already assigned to other categories, just deselect them from the category you want to delete.

▶ Don't assign them to any categories. Notes will display them under "(Not Categorized)".

Changing a Category's Name

To change a category's name, follow these steps:

① Select all the documents in the category (see page 120).

② Access the Categorize dialog box (see Step 2 on the preceding page).

③ Deselect the category (see Step 3 on the preceding page).

④ Type the new category name into the New Categories text box (see "Adding a New Category" on the preceding page).

⑤ Select the OK button.

Moving and Copying Documents

You can move or copy documents between databases using the Windows Clipboard. The table below outlines the Clipboard commands, their effect on the active database, and the keystrokes and SmartIcons that activate them. You can also select the Clipboard commands from the second section of the Edit menu.

Databases and the Clipboard			
Command	**Effect**	**Keys**	**SmartIcon**
Cut	Removes the selected documents from the current database and places them in the Clipboard.	\<Ctrl\> + \<X\>	
Copy	Places the selected documents in the Clipboard.	\<Ctrl\> + \<C\>	
Paste	Places the documents in the Clipboard in the active database.	\<Ctrl\> + \<V\>	

Deleting Documents

To delete documents, follow these steps:

1 Select the Documents

For help selecting documents, see page 119.

2 Mark the Documents

Select "Clear" from the Edit menu. Click on "Edit" in the menu bar, then click on "Clear".

Press \<Delete\> or \<Del\>.

Click on the Edit Clear SmartIcon.

If you selected more than one document, you will receive a prompt similar to this:

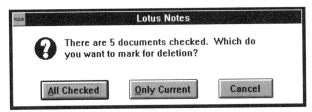

▶ To mark the selected documents, click on the All Checked button, or press <Alt> + <A>.

▶ To mark just the highlighted document, click on the Only Current button, or press <Alt> + <O>.

▶ To not mark any of the documents, click on the Cancel button, or press <Esc>.

Unmarking Documents

To unmark any of the documents, select them, then select "Undo Delete" from the Edit menu.

 Click on "Edit" in the menu bar, then click on "Undo Delete".

Press <Ctrl> + <Z>.

Click on the Edit Undo SmartIcon.

If you selected more than one document, Notes will present a prompt similar to the one shown above.

⃞3 Refresh the View

For help, see "Refreshing the View" on page 42. When you refresh the view, Notes will again ask if you're sure you want to do this:

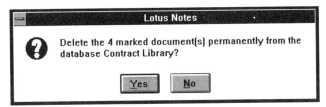

▶ To send the documents to oblivion, click on the Yes button, or press <Alt> + <Y>.

▶To keep the documents around, click on the No button, or press <Alt> + <N>.

Printing Views and Documents

> **Tip:** You can't select a printer from the dialog box that you use to print documents. For help selecting a printer, see page 168.

To print a view, or to print selected documents from a view, follow these steps:

1 Select the Documents

For help selecting documents, see page 119.

2 Access the "File Print" Dialog Box

 Select "Print" from the File menu. Click on "File" in the menu bar, then click on "Print".

Press <Ctrl> + <P>.

Click on the File Print SmartIcon.

File Print Dialog Box

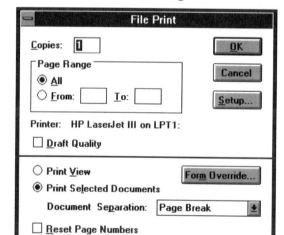

3 Set the Number of Copies

Enter the number of copies you want to print in the Copies text box. To access the text box:

 Double-click in it to overwrite the current number. Click in it to edit.

Press <Alt> + <C>.

4 Set the Page Range

You set the page range from the Page Range group box. You can print the entire document or view, or a range of pages.

Entire Document or View

To print the entire document or view, click on the All option button, or press <Alt> + <A>. Notes will fill the option button.

Range of Pages

To print a range of pages by page number:

① Click on the From option button, or press <Alt> + <F>. Notes will fill the option button.

② Enter the starting page in the From text box. To access the text box, click in it, or press <Tab>.

③ Enter the ending page in the To text box. To access the text box, click in it, or press <Tab> or <Alt> + <T>.

5 Set the "Draft Quality" Option

On most printers, documents print faster with the Draft Quality option on, but the output doesn't look as good. To turn the option on:

 Click on "Draft Quality" or on the small box next to it.

Press <Alt> + <D>.

Notes will fill the Draft Quality check box with an "X".

6 Select View or Documents

You can print the entire contents of the selected documents, or you can print just the view itself.

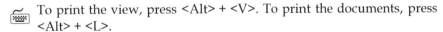 To print the view, click on "Print View" or its option button. To print the documents, click on "Print Selected Documents" or its option button.

To print the view, press <Alt> + <V>. To print the documents, press <Alt> + <L>.

▶ If you're printing the view, skip ahead to Step 8.

▶ If you're printing the documents, continue with the next step.

7 Set the Document Options (Documents Only)

There are three options that only apply when you're printing the entire contents of the documents: Document Separation, Reset Page Numbers, and Form Override.

Document Separation

When you're printing multiple documents, you can specify how Notes separates the documents: with a page break, a blank line, or nothing at all. You make your choice from the Document Separation drop down box.

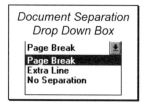

Document Separation Drop Down Box

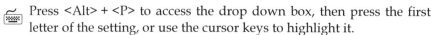

Click on the drop down box to open it, then click on the setting that you want to select.

Press <Alt> + <P> to access the drop down box, then press the first letter of the setting, or use the cursor keys to highlight it.

Reset Page Numbers

The Reset Page Numbers option is only available when the Document Separation option is set to page break. When the Reset Page Numbers check box is filled, Notes starts the page numbering over again at the beginning of each document. When it's empty, Notes numbers all of the printed pages in order, with no distinction between documents. To turn the option on or off:

Click on "Reset Page Numbers" or the check box.

Press <Alt> + <R>.

Form Override

Although you'll probably never want to do this, you can select which form is used to print the information in the selected documents. (You remember forms — they're the templates that you use to create documents.) The apparent intent is to allow you to shape the information in a different way, but unless a new form has been specifically designed for this purpose, it will probably yield garbage. You use the Print Form Override dialog box to select the form.

Print Form Override Dialog Box

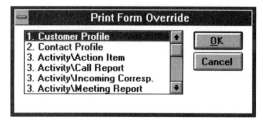

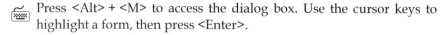

Click on the Form Override button to access the dialog box. Double-click on a form, or click on it once, then click on the OK button. If the list is too long to fit in the box, use the scrollbar to move through it.

Press <Alt> + <M> to access the dialog box. Use the cursor keys to highlight a form, then press <Enter>.

8 Select the "OK" Button

To send the document to the printer, click on the OK button, or press
<Alt> + <O>. To close the dialog box without printing the document, click
on the Cancel button, or press <Esc>.

CHAPTER 10

Searching a Database

Notes offers two types of text searches: plain text and full text.

▶ A **plain text search** provides limited functionality and is slower, but it is also easier to use.

▶ A **full text search** provides powerful functionality (only some of which is discussed here) and is faster, but it requires more expertise, and it requires that the database have an *index*. An index is a separate file that Notes uses to process full text queries.

Performing a Plain Text Search

Performing a plain text search is very similar to searching a document (see "Searching for Text" on page 49). You perform a plain text search from a database view. Follow these steps:

1 Access the "Find" Dialog Box

If you're working with an indexed database, hold down the <Shift> key while you access the dialog box.

🖱 Select "Find" from the Edit menu. Click on "Edit" in the menu bar, then (press <Shift> and) click on "Find".

⌨ Press <Ctrl> + <F> (or press <Ctrl> + <Shift> + <F>).

🖉 Click on the Edit Find SmartIcon (or press <Shift> and click).

Find Dialog Box

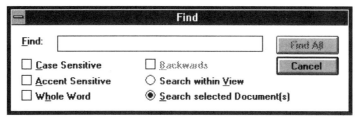

133

2 Enter the Text

Type the text into the Find text box. You can enter special characters (see page 82). To access the text box:

- Double-click in it to overwrite the current text (if any), or click in it to edit the current text.

- Press <Alt> + <F>.

3 Select the Search Type

There are two search types: Search Within View and Search Selected Document(s).

Search Within View

When you select the Search Within View search type, Notes searches the title of every document in the view and ignores the documents' contents.

- Click on "Search within View" or its option button.

- Press <Alt> + <V>.

Search Selected Document(s)

When you select the Search Selected Document(s) search type, Notes searches both the titles and contents of the selected documents. If no documents are selected, Notes searches every document in the view.

- Click on "Search selected Document(s)" or its option button.

- Press <Alt> + <S>.

4 Set the Search Options

There are four search options, each of which are explained below. The Backwards option is only available when you're searching within the view. You turn an option on or off by clicking on its label or its check box, or by pressing <Alt> plus the option's underlined letter.

- **Case Sensitive**
  Searches for text with identical capitalization. For example, ignores "doe" when searching for "Doe".

- **Accent Sensitive**
  Searches for text with identical accents. For example, ignores "ano" when searching for "año".

- **Whole Word**
  Ignores text if partly or entirely contained within another word. For example, ignores "shipping" when searching for "ship".

- **Backwards** *(Search Within View only)*
  Only available when searching within the view. Searches toward the beginning of the view instead of toward the end.

5 Select the "Find All" Button, or the "Find Next" Button

When you're searching within the documents, it's the Find All button. When you're searching within the view, it's the Find Next button.

Click on it.

Press <Alt> + <L> for the Find All button, or <Alt> + <N> for the Find Next button.

6 Keep Searching (Optional)

▶ If you're searching within the view, you may want to keep looking until you find a particular document.

▶ If you're searching the documents, and you have changed views, or have refreshed the current view, you can perform the same search without repeating the previous steps.

Select "Find Next" from the Edit menu. Click on "Edit" in the menu bar, then click on "Find Next".

Press <Ctrl> + <G>.

Click on the Edit Find Again SmartIcon.

Full Text Indices

You can only perform a full text search on databases that have indices. This section covers how you create, review, update, and delete indices.

Indexing a Database

To create an index for a database, follow these steps:

1 Select the Database

You can select an icon in the Workspace, or you can select an open view.

2 Access the "Full Text Create Index" Dialog Box

You access the dialog box by selecting "Create Index" from the File Full
Text Search sub-menu.

Click on "File" in the menu bar, click on "Full Text Search" in the File
menu, then click on "Create Index" in the sub-menu.

Press <Alt> + <F>, press <F>, then press <C>.

Click on the File Full Text Create SmartIcon.

Full Text Create Index Dialog Box

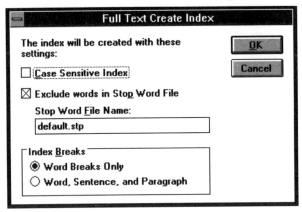

3 Set the "Case Sensitive Index" Option

A case-sensitive index allows you to perform case-sensitive searches. Case-
sensitive indices are typically about five to ten percent larger. To turn the
option on or off:

Click on "Case Sensitive Index" or its option button.

Press <Alt> + <C>.

4 Set the "Stop Word File" Option

A stop word file contains a list of words that you don't want indexed, such
as "the", "a", "an", etc. Using a stop word file decreases the size of the
index, but it prevents users from searching for the listed words. For
example, if the stop word file includes "the", you couldn't search for "The
Satanic Verses" (or for "The Koran" either, for that matter). To turn the
option on or off:

Click on "Exclude words in Stop Word File" or its option button.

Press <Alt> + <P>.

For help changing the stop word file, talk to your technical support person. The words omitted by DEFAULT.STP appear in the following table.

Words Omitted by DEFAULT.STP					
0, 1, 2, etc.	at	from	on	there	whether
a	be	however	or	these	which
all	because	i	other	this	will
after	before	if	out	those	with
also	between	in	since	to	within
an	but	into	such	under	without
and	by	is	than	upon	
are	can	it	that	when	
as	for	of	the	where	

5 | Set the "Index Breaks" Option

Setting the Index Breaks option to Word, Sentence, and Paragraph allows you to search for words that appear within the same sentence or paragraph. For example, you could search for "violence" and "television" in the same sentence. This option increases the size of the index, and may not earn its keep, since the proximity operator "Near" often achieves the desired effect. To set the option:

🖱 Click on the setting you want.

⌨ Press <Alt> + <B>, then use the cursor keys to highlight the setting you want.

6 | Select the "OK" Button

🖱 Click on it.

⌨ Press <Alt> + <O>.

You may receive a prompt asking if you want to index the database now. Select the Yes button. When the index is complete, Notes will present a prompt something like the one shown at right.

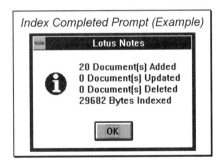

Index Completed Prompt (Example)

Getting Information About an Index

To review a database's index, follow these steps:

1 Select the Database

You can select an icon in the Workspace, or you can select an open view.

2 Access the "Full Text Information" Dialog Box

You access the dialog box by selecting "Information" from the File Full Text Search sub-menu.

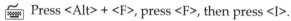 Click on "File" in the menu bar, click on "Full Text Search" in the File menu, then click on "Information" in the sub-menu.

Press <Alt> + <F>, press <F>, then press <I>.

Click on the File Full Text Info SmartIcon.

Full Text Information Dialog Box

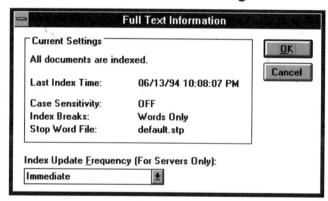

Updating an Index

To update a database's index:

1 Select the Database

You can select an icon in the Workspace, or you can select an open view.

2 Select "Update Index"

You select "Update Index" from the File Full Text Search sub-menu.

Click on "File" in the menu bar, click on "Full Text Search" in the File menu, then click on "Update Index" in the sub-menu.

Press <Alt> + <F>, press <F>, then press <U>.

Click on the File Full Text Update SmartIcon.

▶ If the database does <u>not</u> have an index, you will receive a prompt asking if you want to create one.

▶ If the database <u>does</u> have an index, you will receive a prompt telling you what was done to the index.

Deleting an Index

To delete a database's index:

1 Select the Database

You can select an icon in the Workspace, or you can select an open view.

2 Select "Delete Index"

You select "Delete Index" from the File Full Text Search sub-menu.

Click on "File" in the menu bar, click on "Full Text Search" in the File menu, then click on "Delete Index" in the sub-menu.

Press <Alt> + <F>, press <F>, then press <D>.

▶ If the database does <u>not</u> have an index, you will receive a prompt telling you so.

▶ If the database <u>does</u> have an index, you will receive the following prompt. Select the Yes button to delete the index, or select the No button to save it.

Deleting Index Prompt

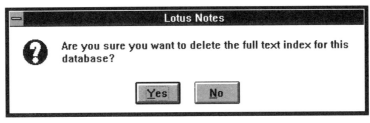

Lotus Notes

Are you sure you want to delete the full text index for this database?

Yes   No

Performing a Full Text Search

A complete discussion of full text searching involves functions and macros and other scary things that are beyond the scope of this book. This section covers the aspects that are well within the novice's grasp, and discusses two methods of performing a full text search — using the Query Builder dialog box, and using the Search Bar to perform a simple search.

The Search Bar is more streamlined than the Query Builder dialog box, but it is also less obvious and requires more expertise. When you use the Query Builder dialog box, Notes loads your query into the Search Bar, which allows you to see how the Search Bar version of your query looks. After you've used the Query Builder a few times, using the Search Bar will become more obvious.

Using the "Query Builder" Dialog Box

To perform a full text search using the Query Builder dialog box, follow these steps:

1 Is the Database Indexed?

The easiest way to tell if a database is indexed is to select "Information" from the File Full Text Search sub-menu (see "Getting Information About an Index" on page 138). If the database isn't indexed, Notes will ask you if you want to index it now.

2 Access the "Query Builder" Dialog Box

 Select "Find" from the Edit menu. Click on "Edit" in the menu bar, then click on "Find".

 Press <Ctrl> + <F>.

Click on the Edit Find SmartIcon.

Query Builder Dialog Box

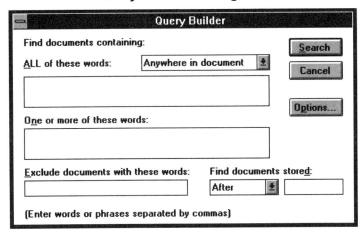

3 | Select Words to Find **All** Of

You can specify words and phrases that the documents must contain. Notes will reject a document if it does not contain every word and phrase in the list.

Entering the Words

You enter the words and phrases in the All of These Words text box, separated by commas (for example, "Bashful, Grumpy, Sneezy"). To access the text box:

 Click in it.

 Press <Alt> + <A>.

Selecting the Word Location

You specify whether the words and phrases can be anywhere in the document or must be near each other. You make your choice from the All of These Words drop down box.

 Click on the drop down box to open it, then click on the selection.

 Press <Alt> + <A> then <Tab> to access the drop down box. Use the cursor keys to highlight a selection.

4 Select Words to Find <u>Some</u> Of

You can specify words and phrases that the documents must contain at least one of. Notes will reject a document if it does not contain at least one of the words and phrases in the list. You enter the words and phrases in the One or More of These Words text box, separated by commas (for example, "treasure, jackpot, buried loot"). To access the text box:

　　🖰 Click in it.

　　⌨ Press <Alt> + <N>.

5 Select Words to Find <u>None</u> Of

You can specify words and phrases that the documents cannot contain. Notes will reject a document if it contains any of the words and phrases in the list. You enter the words and phrases in the Exclude Documents with These Words text box, separated by commas (for example, "filth, dirt, excrement"). To access the text box:

　　🖰 Click in it.

　　⌨ Press <Alt> + <E>.

6 Select Date to Start or End (Optional)

You can specify that the documents must have been created or modified before or after a certain date.

Selecting Before or After

You select before or after from the Find Documents Stored drop down box.

　　🖰 Click on the drop down box to open it, then click on "before" or "after".

　　⌨ Press <Alt> + <D> to access the drop down box, then use the cursor keys to highlight a selection.

Entering the Date

You enter the date in the Find Documents Stored text box. Use the "month/day/year" format. To access the text box:

　　🖰 Click in it.

　　⌨ Press <Alt> + <D>, then <Tab>.

7 Set Search Options

You set the search options from the Search Options dialog box. To access the dialog box, click on the Options button, or press <Alt> + <P>. When you've completed setting the options, click on the OK button or press <Alt> + <O>.

To close the dialog box and cancel the settings, click on the Cancel button or press <Esc>.

Search Options Dialog Box

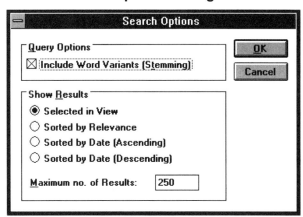

Include Word Variants Option

When the Include Word Variants option is on, Notes automatically adds words that have the same root as those that you specified. For example, if you were excluding documents with the word "smile", Notes would also exclude documents with the word "smiling". The option is on when the check box is filled. To turn it on or off:

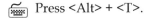 Click on "Include Word Variants (Stemming)" or its check box.

🖮 Press <Alt> + <T>.

Show Results Options

There are four display options for the search results. Each option is explained below. To select a display method:

🖰 Click on it or its option button.

🖮 Press <Alt> + <R>, then use the cursor keys to highlight it.

- **Selected in View**
  Displays the current view and selects the documents that met the search criteria.

- **Sorted by Relevance**
  Displays the search results only, sorted by relevance. Documents are ranked first by the number of matching words or phrases, then by the ratio of matching words or phrases to total length. If two documents have the same number of matches, the shorter document is ranked higher.

- **Sorted by Date (Ascending)**
  Displays the search results only, sorted by date in ascending order.
- **Sorted by Date (Descending)**
  Displays the search results only, sorted by date in descending order.

Maximum Number of Results Option

If your query proves to be imprecise, it may return a large number of documents, which can take quite some time and is usually futile. When you limit the number of documents a search can return, Notes effectively aborts the search if it turns out to be too encompassing. You enter the maximum number of documents that a search can return in the Maximum Number of Results text box. To access the text box:

🖰 Click in it.

⌨ Press <Alt> + <M>.

8 Select the "Search" Button

🖰 Click on it.

⌨ Press <Alt> + <S>.

▶ If Notes finds documents that meet your criteria, it will change the view in accordance with the options that you selected in Step 7, and it will load the query you just created into the Search Bar.

▶ If Notes does not find any documents, the view will remain unchanged, and "no matching documents were found" will be displayed in the Status Bar.

Finding Words and Phrases Within a Document

Notes places a red box around every instance of found text. You can scan through these instances using keystrokes and SmartIcons shown below. The box around the current instance is blue.

Go To	Keys	SmartIcon
Next Instance	<Ctrl> + <+>	
Previous Instance	<Ctrl> + <->	

Performing a Simple Search Using the Search Bar

To perform a simple search using the Search Bar, follow these steps:

1 If Necessary, Index the Database

The easiest way to tell if a database is indexed is to select "Information" from the File Full Text Search sub-menu (see "Getting Information About an Index" on page 138). If the database isn't indexed, Notes will ask you if you want to index it now.

2 Access the Search Bar

You access the Search Bar by selecting "Show Search Bar" from the View menu. Notes places a check mark next to the selection when the Search Bar is displayed. You hide the Search Bar by selecting "Show Search Bar" again. To display or hide the Search Bar:

🖰 Click on "View" in the menu bar, then click on "Show Search Bar".

⌨ Press <Alt> + <V>, then <R>.

Search Bar

3 Enter the Word or Phrase

The cursor will be flashing in the Search text box. Type the word or phrase that you want to search for.

4 Select the "Search" Button

You select the Search button by clicking on it.

▶ If Notes finds documents that meet your criteria, it will change the view to show only the search results, sorted by relevance.

▶ If Notes does not find any documents, the view will remain unchanged, and "no matching documents were found" will be displayed in the Status Bar.

Finding Words and Phrases Within a Document

Notes places a red box around every instance of found text. You can scan through these instances using keystrokes and SmartIcons shown below. The box around the current instance is blue.

Go To	Keys	SmartIcon
Next Instance	<Ctrl> + <+>	🔽
Previous Instance	<Ctrl> + <->	🔼

CHAPTER 11

Notes Mail

This chapter covers the basic features of Notes Mail. Not all organizations that use Notes also use Notes Mail. If you're not sure what type of mail you're using, ask your technical support person.

Notes Mail and Databases

You can think of Notes Mail as a specialized, enhanced set of databases. You and each of your coworkers have individual mail databases, and Notes uses other databases to link them all together. (In actuality it's a bit more complicated, but that's all you need to know to get your work done.)

Mail SmartIcons

Notes has a set of SmartIcons for mail. To use it, click on the SmartIcons button on the Status Bar (see page 13), and select "Mail" from the list. For help using SmartIcons, see "SmartIcons (Tool Bar)" on page 10. For help creating and editing sets of SmartIcons, see "Customizing Your SmartIcons" on page 169.

Using Mail Over a Modem

If you're using Notes remotely — your link to the server is via a modem — then you should:

▶ Create local replicas of your mail database and your organization's address book. See "Creating a Replica" on page 160.

▶ Change your setup to workstation-based mail, and your mail file to the local replica. See "Modifying Your Mail Setup" below.

Modifying Your Mail Setup

Once you've created the local replicas (see above), you should make some changes to your mail setup. Follow these steps:

1 Get Your Local Mail Database's File Name

① If the local replica is open, make it active. If it isn't, select its icon.

② Select "Database" from the File menu, then select "Information" from the sub-menu. Notes will open the Database Information dialog box.

③ Copy down the file name exactly as it appears in the dialog box, including any path information. For example, if the dialog box shows "MAIL\MYMAIL.NSF", make sure you include "MAIL\".

④ Close the Database Information dialog box. Click on the Cancel button or press <Esc>.

2 Access the "Mail Setup" Dialog Box

Select "Setup" from the Tools menu, then select "Mail" from the sub-menu.

Mail Setup Dialog Box (Example)

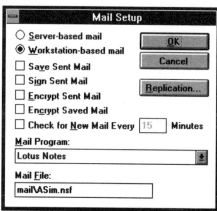

3 **Select "Workstation-Based Mail"**

🖑 Click on it.

⌨ Press <Alt> + <W>.

4 **Check the Contents of the "Mail File" Text Box**

If it differs from the file name in the Database Information dialog box, press <Alt> + <F> and overwrite the existing file name. Make sure that the two match exactly, including any path information.

5 **Select the "OK" Button**

🖑 Click on it.

⌨ Press <Alt> + <O>.

The MAIL.BOX Database

When you send mail from a remote setup, Notes places the mail in a local database called "MAIL.BOX". Notes transfers the contents of MAIL.BOX to the server when you perform replication with the Transfer Outgoing Mail option turned on (see "Performing Replication" on page 161).

Notes creates MAIL.BOX automatically the first time you send mail. If it isn't in your Workspace, it's a good idea to put it there. If you can't remember if you've sent something, or are unsure if you remembered to transfer it (via replication), you can open the database and have a look. You can also delete messages if you decide that you don't want to send them (a particularly handy feature if you happen to be hotheaded).

Opening Your Mail

There are two ways to open your mail: you can open your mail database, or you can scan your unread mail. If you're using Notes remotely — your link to the server is via a modem — then you'll need to perform replication to receive your mail. See "Performing Replication" on page 161.

Opening Your Mail Database

You can open your mail database and use the features discussed in previous chapters to read the documents contained therein. You can open the database just like you would any other, or you can select "Open" from the Mail menu.

Mail
Database
Icon

Click on "Mail" in the menu bar, then click on "Open".

Press <Alt> + <M>, then <O>.

Click on the Mail Open SmartIcon.

Scanning Your Unread Mail

To scan your unread mail:

Select "Scan Unread" from the Mail menu. Click on "Mail" in the menu bar, then click on "Scan Unread".

Press <Ctrl> + <M>.

Click on the Mail Scan Unread SmartIcon.

Writing Mail

Writing mail is much like creating any other document. To create and send a mail document, follow these steps:

1 Select a Mail Form

You use the Mail Compose sub-menu to select a mail form. The "Custom Forms" selection opens a dialog box that you can use to select a custom mail form, if there are any available on your server.

Click on "Mail" in the menu bar, click on "Compose" in the Mail menu, then click on a selection.

Press <Alt> + <M>, then <C>, then press the selection's underlined letter, or use the cursor keys to highlight it and press <Enter>.

You can select the mail memo form by clicking on the Mail Memo SmartIcon.

2 Address the Document

This may seem a little backward — in real, physical mail you generally address the letter last — but since most mail forms open up with the insertion point in the "To" field, you might as well start there.

If you know the person's address, you can type it in directly, but that's pretty risky, since you may spell it wrong or forget part of the long, arcane prefix that generally begins a network address. Luckily, there's an easier way: you can use an address book. (For more help with address books, see the following page.)

Opening the Address Book Window

You use an address book from an Address Book window, which is a specialized view that is used only for address books. To open the window:

Select Address from the Mail menu. Click on "Mail" in the menu bar, then click on "Address".

If the form has an Address button (or some contraction, like "Addr Butn"), click on it.

Select "Address" from the Mail menu. Press <Alt> + <M>, then <A>.

Click on the Mail Address SmartIcon.

Address Book Window (Example)

Changing the Address Book

Notes automatically opens the address book that was used last. You change the address book from the Address Book drop down box (displaying "Sim's Address Book" above). Click on the drop down box to open it, then click on the book that you want.

Selecting Addressees

You select an addressee just like you select a document in a conventional database: click next to him or her in the marker bar, or use the cursor keys to highlight the row and press <Spacebar>. You can find an addressee by typing his last name. When you're done selecting addressees, click on the Add button.

Closing the Address Book Window

To close the Address Book window:

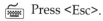 Double-click on the Control box, which occupies the window's upper left corner.

Press <Esc>.

3 Write the Message (Fill the Fields)

How you finish the document depends on its fields and features. See "Editing Documents" on page 55.

4 Send the Document

Select "Send" from the Mail menu. Click on "Mail" in the menu bar, then click on "Send".

If the document has a Send button, click on it.

Select "Send" from the Mail menu. Press <Alt> + <M>, then <S>.

Click on the Mail Send SmartIcon.

Where you go from here depends on your mail template. You may receive a prompt or prompts asking you to make more decisions about the fate of your newly-written mail document. If in doubt, try pressing <F1> to see if there's any on-line help available for the prompt.

Using Mail Over a Modem

If you're using Notes remotely and replicating your mail databases, then you'll need to perform replication to send your mail. See "The MAIL.BOX Database" on page 149 and "Performing Replication" on page 161.

Address Books

Check your Workspace for address book databases, which should have icons like the one shown at right. Start on the page that holds your mail database. Chances are that you have at least two address books, one for your organization, and one for you. If not, you should add your organization's address book to your Workspace, and you may want to create an address book of your own.

Address Book Icon

Finding Your Organization's Address Book

You can probably find your organization's address book on your main server. If not, contact your technical support person for help, or ask a knowledgeable coworker.

Creating a Personal Address Book

If you can't find a personal address book in your Workspace, you can make one yourself. Just create a database using the Name & Address Book template. For help creating a new database, see page 29. Once you've done that, you can copy entries out of your organization's address book and paste them into your new personal address book. See "Moving and Copying Documents" on page 126.

Forwarding Documents

To forward documents, follow these steps:

1 Select the Documents

For help selecting documents, see page 119.

2 Select "Forward" from the "Mail" Menu

Click on "Mail" in the menu bar, then click on "Forward".

Press <Alt> + <M>, then <F>.

Click on the Mail Forward SmartIcon.

Notes will create a new mail memo and insert the selected documents in the memo's body.

3 Address the Document

If you know the person's address, you can type it in directly, or you can use an address book. (For more help with address books, see the preceding page.)

Opening the Address Book Window

You use an address book from an Address Book window, which is a specialized view that is used only for address books. To open the window:

Select "Address" from the Mail menu. Click on "Mail" in the menu bar, then click on "Address".

If the form has an Address button (or some contraction, like "Addr Butn"), click on it.

Select "Address" from the Mail menu. Press <Alt> + <M>, then <A>.

Click on the Mail Address SmartIcon.

Address Book Window (Example)

Mail Address		
To: ⬇	[text field] Add Open	⬆
Sim's Address Book ⬇	☐ By Organization	
Name		
🗒 Gross, Jack		
📑 LocalDomainServers		
🗒 Lock, Owen		
📑 OtherDomainServers		
🗒 Sterns, Stephen H.		⬇

Changing the Address Book

Notes automatically opens the address book that was used last. You change the address book from the Address Book drop down box (displaying "Sim's Address Book" above). Click on the drop down box to open it, then click on the book that you want.

Selecting Addressees

You select an addressee just like you select a document in a conventional database: click next to him or her in the marker bar, or use the cursor keys to highlight the row and press <Spacebar>. You can find an addressee by typing his last name. When you're done selecting addressees, click on the Add button.

Closing the Address Book Window

To close the Address Book window:

🖱 Double-click on the Control box (upper left corner).

⌨ Press <Esc>.

4 Send the Document

🖱 Select "Send" from the Mail menu. Click on "Mail" in the menu bar, then click on "Send".

🖱 If the document has a Send button, click on it.

⌨ Select "Send" from the Mail menu. Press <Alt> + <M>, then <S>.

 Click on the Mail Send SmartIcon.

Where you go from here depends on your mail template. You may receive a prompt or prompts asking you to make more decisions about the fate of your newly-written mail document. If in doubt, try pressing <F1> to see if there's any on-line help available for the prompt.

Using Mail Over a Modem

If you're using Notes remotely and replicating your mail databases, then you'll need to perform replication to send your mail. See "The MAIL.BOX Database" on page 149 and "Performing Replication" on page 161.

CHAPTER 12

Notes Remote: Using a Modem

Getting Set Up

For Notes to work remotely, it needs to know a few things:

- Your user ID, which is probably on a diskette given to you by your technical support person.
- Your password.
- Your Home server name.
- The server's telephone number.

If you've already installed Notes on your computer and now you want to tell it your ID, you may encounter some problems. Our experience has been pretty discouraging. We recommend removing Notes completely — including NOTES.INI, which should be in your Windows directory — and reinstalling it. Follow Notes' standard installation procedure for a remote workstation, which calls for you to provide the file that contains your user ID.

Remote SmartIcons

Notes has a set of SmartIcons for working remotely. To use it, click on the SmartIcons button on the Status Bar (see page 13), and select "Remote" from the list. For help using SmartIcons, see "SmartIcons (Tool Bar)" on page 10. For help creating and editing sets of SmartIcons, see "Customizing Your SmartIcons" on page 169.

Calling a Server

To dial in to a server, follow these steps:

1 Access the "Call Server" Dialog Box

To access the dialog box, select "Call" from the Tools menu.

🖐 Click on "Tools" in the menu bar, then click on "Call".

⌨ Press <Alt> + <O>, then <A>.

📠 Click on the Tools Call SmartIcon.

If you haven't called in yet this session, you will be prompted to enter your password. Type it in and press <Enter>. Notes will open the Call Server dialog box.

Call Server Dialog Box

```
┌─────────────────────────────────────────────────────────┐
│ ─                       Call Server                      │
│  Server:                                                 │
│  BallNotes_1/Ballantine/RandomHouse        │ Auto Dial  ││
│                                            │            ││
│                                            │ Manual Dial││
│                                            │            ││
│                                            │  Cancel    ││
│  Dialing Prefix:        Phone Number:                    │
│  ┌──────────────┐       │ 1-800-416-4191 │  │Call Setup...│
│  Port:                                                   │
│  COM2                   ┌────────────────────┐           │
│                         │ Additional Setup... │          │
│                         Dial Timeout [      ] seconds    │
│                         Hangup if idle for [    ] minutes│
└─────────────────────────────────────────────────────────┘
```

2 Select the Server

Chances are that you're setup with only one server. If so, click on the Auto Dial button, or press <Enter>. If not:

🖐 Double-click on the server that you want to use. If the list is too long to fit in the box, use the scroll bar to move through it.

⌨ Press <Alt> + <S> to access the list box. Use the cursor keys to highlight the server, then press <Enter>.

Notes will dial in to the selected server, and will display a series of messages on the Status Bar detailing its progress. When the call goes through, or if it fails, Notes will close the Call Server dialog box.

Hanging Up

To disconnect from a server, follow these steps:

1 Access the "Hang Up" Dialog Box

To access the dialog box, select "Hang Up" from the Tools menu.

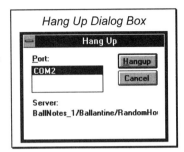

Hang Up Dialog Box

 Click on "Tools" in the menu bar, then click on "Hang Up".

Press <Alt> + <O>, then <H>.

Click on the Tools Hang Up SmartIcon.

2 Select the Port

Chances are that you're setup with only one port. If so, it will already be selected. If not:

Click on the port that you want to disconnect.

Press <Alt> + <P> to access the list box. Use the cursor keys to select the port.

3 Select the "Hang Up" Button

Click on it.

Press <Alt> + <H>.

What Is Replication?

It's not always practical for everyone to use the same copy of a given database. Running Notes over a modem is a prime example: if you use a database that's on the server, you have to execute your commands over the connecting telephone line, a slow and potentially expensive process. *Replication* solves this problem by maintaining copies, called *replicas*, of the shared database. The changes that users make to each replica are periodically transmitted to the shared database and to the other replicas.

When Should I Use Replication?

If you're using Notes remotely and are going to be working with a database for anything more than a few minutes, it's probably a good idea to create a local replica. The extra time spent to create the replica and transmit your changes will be more than compensated by the time saved in actually making your changes.

Creating a Replica

To create a local replica of a shared database, follow these steps:

1 Select a Workspace Page

Activate the Workspace window and select a page for the replica's icon.

2 Call the Server

See "Calling a Server" on page 158.

3 Add the Shared Database's Icon

See "Adding an Icon" on page 26. Make sure that the database's icon is selected before going on to the next step. When you're done creating the replica, you can delete the shared database's icon, but unless you're running out of room in your Workspace, there's no harm in keeping it around.

4 Access the "New Replica" Dialog Box

To access the dialog box (see diagram on the following page), select "New Replica" from the File menu.

🖱 Click on "File" in the menu bar, then click on "New Replica".

⌨ Press <Alt> + <F>, then <R>.

▧ Click on the File New Replica SmartIcon.

5 Set the "Initialize and Copy" Option to "Now"

🖱 Click on "Now" or its option button.

⌨ Press <Alt> + <I>, then press <↑> or <↓>.

New Replica Dialog Box (Example)

```
┌─────────────────────────────────────────────────────────────┐
│ ═                      New Replica                            │
├─────────────────────────────────────────────────────────────┤
│  ┌─Original Database──────────────────────────┐   ┌────────┐ │
│  │ Server:                                     │   │  New   │ │
│  │ ┌──────────────────────────────────┐ ┌──┐  │   └────────┘ │
│  │ │ BallNotes_1/Ballantine/RandomHo  │ │ ± │  │   ┌────────┐ │
│  │ └──────────────────────────────────┘ └──┘  │   │ Cancel │ │
│  │ Filename:                                   │   └────────┘ │
│  │ ┌──────────────────────────────────┐        │             │
│  │ │ BALLDISC.NSF                     │        │             │
│  │ └──────────────────────────────────┘        │             │
│  └─────────────────────────────────────────────┘             │
│  ┌─New Replica────────────────────────────────┐              │
│  │ Server:                                     │              │
│  │ ┌──────────────────────────────────┐ ┌──┐  │ ┌─Initialize and Copy─┐
│  │ │ Local                            │ │ ± │  │ │  ○ Now              │
│  │ └──────────────────────────────────┘ └──┘  │ │  ◉ First replication│
│  │ Filename:                                   │ └─────────────────────┘
│  │ ┌──────────────────────────────────┐        │              │
│  │ │ BALLDISC.NSF                     │        │              │
│  │ └──────────────────────────────────┘        │              │
│  └─────────────────────────────────────────────┘              │
│   ⊠ Replicate Access Control List                             │
│   ☐ Only Replicate documents saved in the last ┌──┐ days     │
│                                                 │90│          │
│                                                 └──┘          │
└─────────────────────────────────────────────────────────────┘
```

6 │ Select the "New" Button

🖱 Click on it.

⌨ Press <Alt> + <N>.

Notes will create the new replica and add its icon to the Workspace.

Performing Replication

Performing replication passes your changes to the shared database, and/or receives other user's changes from the shared database. To perform replication, follow the steps below.

1 │ Select the Databases (Optional)

If you want to send and/or receive changes for all of your replicas, you don't have to select them. If you want to perform replication for specific databases, select their icons.

Sending and Receiving Notes Mail

If you're sending Notes Mail, you don't have to select your mail database, but if you want to receive your mail, you do. For more help with Notes Mail, see page 147.

2 Call the Server

See "Calling a Server" on page 158.

3 Access the "Tools Replicate" Dialog Box

To access the dialog box, select "Replicate" from the Tools menu.

Click on "Tools" in the menu bar, then click on "Replicate".

Press <Alt> + <O>, then <E>.

Click on the Tools Replicate SmartIcon.

Tools Replicate Dialog Box

4 Select "Replicate" Options

The Replicate options control which databases will be replicated and what will be copied. An explanation of each option follows. To turn an option on or off:

Click on its text or its option button.

Press <Alt> plus its underlined letter.

- **All Databases in Common**
  Send and/or receive changes for all replicas of shared databases that are on the current server. This option and the next option are mutually exclusive.

- **Selected Database(s)**
  Send and/or receive changes for the selected databases only. This option and the previous option are mutually exclusive.

- **Receive Documents from Server**
  Receive changes for specified databases (see previous two options).

- **Send Documents to Server**
  Send changes for specified databases (see first two options).

- **Replicate Database Templates**
  Send and/or receive changes to the database's templates.

- **Exchange Document Read Marks**
  Send and/or receive documents' read/unread status.

5 | Select Other Options

An explanation of each remaining option follows. To turn an option on or off:

🖱 Click on its text or its option button.

⌨ Press <Alt> plus its underlined letter.

- **Transfer Outgoing Mail**
  If you're using Notes Mail, and have taken our advice and are using workstation-based mail (see "Modifying Your Mail Setup" on page 148), then you want to turn this option on if there is any pending correspondence in MAIL.BOX (see "The MAIL.BOX Database" on page 149). When Notes has completed sending the documents, it will delete them from MAIL.BOX.

- **Hang Up When Done**
  When Notes has finished replicating, it will automatically disconnect from the server.

- **Run in Background**
  Perform replication in the background so that you can use your computer to do other work.

6 | Select the "OK" Button

🖱 Click on it.

⌨ Press <Alt> + <O>.

CHAPTER 13

Modifying Your Setup

Changing Your Password

To change your password, follow these steps:

1 Access the "Enter Password" Dialog Box

To open the dialog box:

Click on "Tools" in the menu bar, then click on "User ID" in the Tools menu. Click on "Password" in the User ID sub-menu, then click on "Set".

Press <Alt> + <O>, then <I>, <P>, and <S>.

Enter Password Dialog Box

```
┌─────────────────────────────────────────────────┐
│ ─              Enter Password                     │
│                                                   │
│ Enter the password for Al Sim/External/RandomHouse:  ┌──────┐ │
│                                                   │  OK  │ │
│                                                   ├──────┤ │
│                                                   │Cancel│ │
│ ┌───────────────────────────────────────┐        └──────┘ │
│ └───────────────────────────────────────┘                 │
│ Automatically log off after  ┌────┐ minutes of inactivity │
│                              └────┘                        │
└─────────────────────────────────────────────────┘
```

2 Enter Your Current Password

Type your current password and press <Enter>. Notes will close the dialog box and open the first version of the Set Password dialog box.

Set Password Dialog Box, Version #1 (Example)

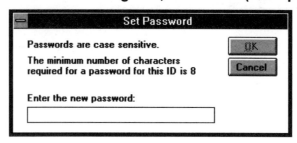

③ Enter Your New Password

Type your new password, which must be at least the number of characters posted in the first version of the Set Password dialog box (eight in the example above), and no more than thirty-one characters. Passwords are case-sensitive. When you're done, press <Enter>. If you've obeyed the rules, Notes will close the first version of the Set Password dialog box and open the second version. If not, it will prompt you to try again.

Set Password Dialog Box, Version #2

④ Enter Your New Password Again

Type your new password again, and press <Enter> one more time. If you enter it correctly, Notes will close the Set Password dialog box. Your new password is now official. If you enter it incorrectly, Notes will prompt you to try again.

Date and Time Settings

You set the date and time information from the Location Setup dialog box. To access the dialog box, select "Location" from the Tools Setup sub-menu.

Click on "Tools" in the menu bar, click on "Setup" in the Tools menu, then click on "Location".

Press <Alt> + <O>, then <S>, and then <L>.

Click on the Tools Setup Location SmartIcon.

Location Setup Dialog Box

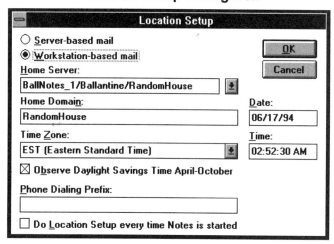

Enter the following information, then click on the OK button, or press <Alt> + <O>.

Time Zone

You set the time zone from the Time Zone drop down box.

Click on the drop down box, then click on the correct zone. Use the scroll bar to move through the list.

Press <Alt> + <Z>, then press the first letter of the zone that you want to select. Keep pressing it until the correct zone is displayed.

Daylight Savings Time

The Observe Daylight Savings Time option is on when the check box is filled. To turn the option on or off:

Click on the text or the check box.

Press <Alt> + <B>.

Date

You type the date into the Date text box. Use the Month/Day/Year format. To access the text box:

Double-click in it to overwrite the current date setting. Click in it once to edit the current setting.

Press <Alt> + <D>.

Time

You type the time into the Time text box. Use the Hours:Minutes:Seconds AM/PM format. To access the text box:

Double-click in it to overwrite the current time setting. Click in it once to edit the current setting.

Press <Alt> + <T>.

Selecting a Printer

You select a printer from the Print Setup dialog box. To access the dialog box, select "Print Setup" from the File menu.

Click on "File" in the menu bar, then click on "Print Setup".

Press <Alt> + <F>, then <T>.

Click on the File Print Setup SmartIcon.

Print Setup Dialog Box

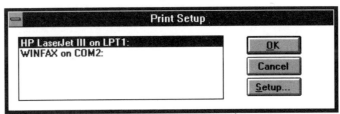

To select a printer:

Click on it in the list box, then click on the OK button. If the list is too long to fit in the box, use the scroll bar to move through it.

Use the cursor keys to highlight it, or press its first letter until it's highlighted. Press <Alt> + <O>.

Customizing Your SmartIcons

> **Please Note:** Since you use SmartIcons with the mouse, this section assumes that you like using the mouse, and dispenses with instructions for the keyboard.

You customize your SmartIcons from the SmartIcons dialog box. To access the dialog box, select "SmartIcons" from the Tools menu.

Click on "Tools" in the menu bar, then click on "SmartIcons".

Click on the Tools SmartIcons SmartIcon.

SmartIcons Dialog Box

SmartIcons			?
Available icons:	Default Set		**OK**
[Spacer]	File Save		**Cancel**
Design Doc Info	File Open Database		
Design Form Attributes	File Print		**Position:**
Design Form Field Definition	Edit Undo		Top
Design Form New Field	Edit Cut		**Edit Icon...**
Design Form Use Shared Field	Edit Copy		
Design Icon	Edit Paste		**Save Set...**
Design Synopsis	Edit Clear		**Delete Set...**
Design View Attributes	Navigate Next		
Design View Column Definition			**Icon Size...**

> **Tip:** Many of the SmartIcon dialog boxes (like the one shown above) have a small button containing a question mark in the upper right hand corner (see diagram at right). Clicking on the button accesses Notes on-line help for SmartIcons. You may have to click on a few doclinks to find the stuff that pertains to what you're doing.

Help Button

Saving Your Changes

Notes applies the changes that you've made when you click on the OK button. To close the dialog box without saving your changes, click on the Cancel button.

Changing the Size of Your SmartIcons

To change the size of your SmartIcons, click on the Icon Size button. Notes will open the Icon Size dialog box. Click on small, medium, or large. Notes will display an example of the size in the lower right corner of the dialog box. When you've found the size you like, click on the OK button.

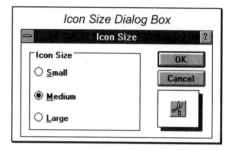

Changing the Position of Your SmartIcons

To change the position of your SmartIcons, click on the Position drop down box, then click on the location that you want.

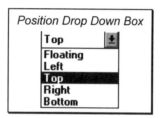

Editing a Set of SmartIcons

To select a set of SmartIcons to edit, click on the Set drop down box, then click on the set.

Adding a SmartIcon or a Space
To add a SmartIcon or a space, drag it from the Available Icons list box (on the left) to the Current Set list box (on the right). Notes positions the icon wherever you drop it.

Rearranging the SmartIcons and Spaces
You rearrange the current set's SmartIcons and spaces by dragging and dropping in the Current Set list box (the one on the right).

Removing a SmartIcon or a Space
To remove a SmartIcon or a space, drag it out of the Current Set list box (the one on the right) and drop it anywhere.

Creating a New Set of SmartIcons

To create a new set of SmartIcons, you copy an existing set and edit it. Follow these steps:

1 Select the Set to Copy

Use the Set drop down box to select the set of SmartIcons that you want to copy.

2 Click On the "Save Set" Button

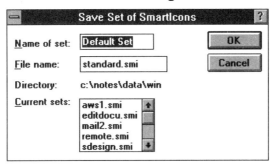

Notes will open the Save Set dialog box. You use the dialog box to save the set that you just selected under a new name.

Save Set Dialog Box

3 Enter the New Name

Type the new name of fifteen characters or less into the Name of Set text box, then press <Enter>. Notes will try to assign the set a file name equaling the first eight characters of the set's name plus ".SMI". If it succeeds, it will close the dialog box and you're done. If it fails, you'll receive a prompt something like this:

Set File Name Failure Prompt (Example)

▶ Click on the Yes button to overwrite the existing set.

▶ Click on the No button to return to the Save Set dialog box. You can try entering a different name for the new set, or you can edit the contents of the File Name text box.

4 Edit the New Set

When you return to the SmartIcon dialog box, the new set will be selected. For more help, see "Editing a Set of SmartIcons" on page 170.

Deleting Sets of SmartIcons

To delete one or more sets of SmartIcons, click on the Delete Set button. Notes will open the Delete Sets dialog box. Click on each set that you want to delete, then click on the OK button.

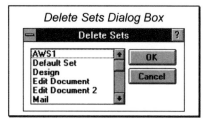

Delete Sets Dialog Box

CHAPTER 14

Odds and Ends

Manipulating Secondary Windows

Notes has three different types of secondary windows:

- Database Windows
- Document Windows
- The Workspace Window

Arranging All of the Secondary Windows

The four selections at the top of the Windows menu reposition all of the open secondary windows. The following table explains what each selection does.

Windows Menu Positioning Selections	
Selection	**Effect**
Tile	Supposed to arrange the non-minimized secondary windows horizontally, one below the other, without any overlap. Succeeds on everything but the Workspace. If Workspace is currently maximized, it is reduced but not tiled. If Workspace is not maximized, it isn't affected at all.
Cascade	Arranges the non-minimized secondary windows in an overlapping stack. All windows except the Workspace are resized identically. Workspace is restored to its last non-maximized state.
Minimize All	This is the only selection that behaves according to Windows standards. Reduces all secondary windows to icons.
Maximize All	Maximizes the active secondary window, then maximizes each of the other open secondary windows as you select them. If you minimize or restore the active window, you'll find that the other windows have not been repositioned or resized.

Positioning a Window with the Mouse

Double-clicking on the text display section of a secondary window's title bar switches the window between its maximized and normal states. At the right end of the title bar are the secondary window's positioning buttons. You select a button by clicking on it. When a window is maximized, the Maximize and Minimize buttons are replaced by the Restore button.

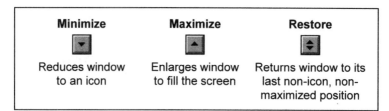

Minimize	**Maximize**	**Restore**
Reduces window to an icon	Enlarges window to fill the screen	Returns window to its last non-icon, non-maximized position

Moving a Secondary Window with the Mouse

When a secondary window is not maximized or minimized, you can move it within Notes' main window.

① Point at the text display section of the title bar.

② Press and hold the primary mouse button.

③ Drag the window to its new location by moving the mouse.

④ Release the mouse button.

Sizing a Secondary Window with the Mouse

When a secondary window is not maximized or minimized, you can change its size by dragging a side or a corner.

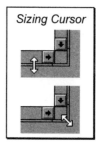

Sizing Cursor

① Point at the side or corner that you want to move. The cursor will change to a two-headed arrow.

② Press and hold the primary mouse button.

③ Drag the side or corner to its new location by moving the mouse.

④ Release the mouse button.

Positioning a Secondary Window with the Keyboard

At the left end of a secondary window's title bar is the Control box. You use the Control box to access the Secondary Window Control menu. You open the Control menu by clicking on the box, or by pressing <Alt> + <Spacebar>.

You can use the Control menu to position the secondary window, to close it, or to switch to the next secondary window. You choose a menu selection by pressing its underlined letter, or using the cursor keys to highlight it and pressing <Enter>.

The Control menu also lists the hot keys that perform the same commands. The following table explains each command.

Control Box

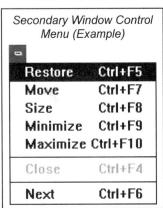

Secondary Window Control Menu (Example)

Accessing Positioning Commands with the Keyboard		
Command	**Description**	**Keys**
Restore	Returns window to its last non-icon, non-maximized size and position	<Ctrl> + <F5>
Move	Puts window in Move Mode. See "Moving a Secondary Window with the Keyboard" on the following page.	<Ctrl> + <F7>
Size	Puts window in Size Mode. See "Sizing a Secondary Window with the Keyboard" on the following page.	<Ctrl> + <F8>
Minimize	Reduces window to an icon	<Ctrl> + <F9>
Maximize	Enlarges window to fill the available space	<Ctrl> + <F10>
Close	Closes the window	<Ctrl> + <F4>
Next	Activates the next secondary window as listed on the Windows menu	<Ctrl> + <F6>

Moving a Secondary Window with the Keyboard

When a secondary window is not maximized or minimized, you can move it within Notes' main window. Follow these steps:

1 Select the "Move" Command

Positioning
Cursor

Press <Ctrl> + <F7>, or select "Move" from the Control menu (see previous page). The cursor will change to a four-headed arrow.

2 Use the Arrow Keys to Move the Window

When you press an arrow key, the cursor will switch back to the default, and a box will appear under the cursor. The box indicates where the window will go.

3 Press <Enter>

When you press <Enter>, Notes will move the window to the new spot. If you change your mind and want to leave the window where it is, press <Esc> instead of <Enter>.

Sizing a Secondary Window with the Keyboard

When a secondary window is not maximized or minimized, you can change its size by moving a side or a corner. Follow these steps:

1 Select the "Size" Command

Positioning
Cursor

Press <Ctrl> + <F8>, or select "Size" from the Control menu (see previous page). The cursor will change to a four-headed arrow.

2 Select a Side or Corner of the Window

Use the arrow keys to select a side or corner of the window (see table below). The cursor will switch to a two-headed arrow.

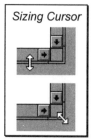

Sizing Cursor

Keys	Selects	Keys	Selects
<←>	Left Side	<←> then <↑>	Upper Left Corner
<→>	Right Side	<←> then <↓>	Lower Left Corner
<↑>	Top	<→> then <↑>	Upper Right Corner
<↓>	Bottom	<→> then <↓>	Lower Right Corner

③ Use the Arrow Keys to Position the Side or Corner

Use the arrow keys to place the side or corner in the correct position.

④ Press <Enter>

When you press <Enter>, Notes will resize the window. If you change your mind and want to leave the window where it is, press <Esc> instead.

Closing a Secondary Window

> **Please Note:** You cannot close the Workspace window.

Select "Close Window" from the File menu. Click on "File" in the menu bar, then click on "Close Window".

Double-click on the window's Control box ().

Double-click in the window with the secondary mouse button.

Press <Esc>.

Press <Ctrl> + <W>.

Press <Ctrl> + <F4>.

Stopping Notes

To stop Notes from completing a task, press <Ctrl> + <Break>. The message "operation stopped at your request" will appear on the Status Bar. In some cases, the stop request won't be fast enough, and Notes will complete the task anyway.

Using Notes Help

The following table lists five ways to access Notes Help. Notes also provides simple help for menu selections, SmartIcons, and fields. See "What Does This Menu Selection Do?" on page 10, "What Does This SmartIcon Do?" on page 10, and "Getting Help with Fields" on page 55.

Accessing Notes Help	
Feature	**Description**
⌨ <F1>	Pressing <F1> accesses help with the window or dialog box that you are currently using.
❓	Clicking on the Help SmartIcon accesses help with the window that you are currently using.
Help *or* ❓	Clicking on a help button accesses help for the dialog box or document that contains the button.
<u>H</u>elp	The ten selections on the Help menu (see the following page) access help on a variety of topics.
📑	You can open the help database and look for information on a topic or task. See "Using the Help Database" on the following page.

Help Windows

When you access a Notes Help topic, Notes opens one of two window types: a floating window or a standard document window. A floating help window appears on top of Notes and automatically disappears when you resume your work or switch to another application. You can also close a floating window by double-clicking on its title bar.

Floating Help Window (Example)

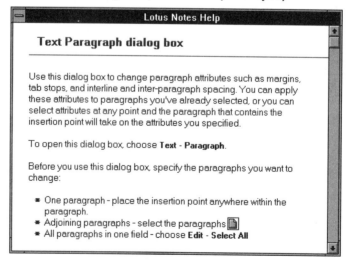

The "Help" Menu

The Help menu contains ten selections. The first six access information about using Notes. The next two access information about the current database. The last two access information about your current release of Notes.

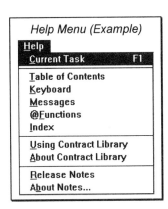

Help Menu (Example)

When you highlight a menu selection, Notes displays a brief description of what it does in the title bar. See "What Does This Menu Selection Do?" on page 10.

To choose a Help menu selection:

🖱️ Click on "Help" in the menu bar, then click on the selection.

⌨️ Press <Alt> + <H>, then press the selection's underlined letter.

Using the Help Database

The Notes help database is entitled "Notes Help Release 3", and its file name is HELP.NSF. You can open the database like any other, or you can select "Table of Contents" or "Index" from the Help menu (see above). You can look for information by manipulating one of the database's views, which are described below, or you can use Notes search capabilities. See "Searching a Database" on page 133.

Table of Contents View

Breaks information into eight major categories and one level of sub-categories. Major categories are (in order):

① What Is Notes
② Notes Basics
③ Using Mail
④ Security
⑤ Sharing Information with Other Applications
⑥ Dial-Up Notes
⑦ Designing Databases
⑧ Administrator Tasks

Messages View

Lists help topics for error messages in alphabetical order. You can search the list by typing the text of a message. For example, typing "co" highlights "Could not open the ID file".

> **Tip:** Using this database is probably going about things the hard way. To get help with an error message that is displayed on your screen, press <F1>.

@Functions View

Lists help topics for @Functions in alphabetical order. (You use @Functions to customize Notes; they are not covered in this book.) You can search the list by typing a function's name without the "@". For example, typing "db" highlights "DbColumn".

Release Notes View

Lists only the Release Notes Database document, which provides a brief description of the Release Notes database.

Index View

Lists topic categories in alphabetical order. You can search the list by typing the title of a category. For example, typing "fo" highlights "Focus, Changing".

Common Limits

Item	Limit
Database, maximum size	1 gigabyte
Database title, maximum length	32 characters
Margin, maximum value	45.51
Page breaks, maximum in a document	Unlimited
Paragraph styles, maximum unique	64,000
Paragraphs, maximum in a document	21,509
Password, maximum length	31 characters
Point size, maximum	218
Printing, maximum copies at one time	65,535
SmartIcon set, maximum title length	15 characters
Table, maximum columns	64
Table, maximum rows	255
View response level, maximum documents	300,000
View response levels, maximum	31 levels
Windows, maximum open	9

Glossary

> **Please Note:** If a defined term is used in another term's definition, the referenced term is italicized.

About Database Document

An About Database Document is a *document* that contains information about a *database's* purpose.

Accelerator Keys

Accelerator keys are a simultaneous combination of keys that accesses a feature or function. Synonyms: *hot keys, short-cut keys*.

Access Control List

A *database's* Access Control List specifies which users can open the database and what tasks they can perform. Access Control Lists have two elements, *access levels* and *access roles*, both of which are set by the database's designer or its manager.

Access Levels

A *database's* access levels determine what operations can be performed by which users.

Access Roles

Access roles determine which users have access to which forms or *views*.

Active Window

The active window is the *window* that is currently receiving keyboard input.

Button

Buttons appear in *dialog boxes* and *documents*. They appear raised and contain a label or picture. You activate a button by *clicking* on it, or by pressing its *hot keys*, which are usually <Alt> plus the label's underlined letter. When a button has a thick border, like the one in the example at right, you can activate it by pressing <Enter>.

Button (Example)

Click/Clicking

You click on something by using the mouse to place the cursor over the item and pressing the *primary mouse button* once. For most users, the primary mouse button is the one on the left. If you're left-handed, it may be on the right.

Combo Box

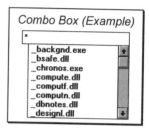

A combo box is a hybrid of a *text box* and a *list box*, hence the name. The text section acts upon the list section, allowing you to narrow the list or find an entry by typing text. The text section is the small rectangle at the top of the combo box, and the list section is the larger rectangle at the bottom.

Compose Sequence

A compose sequence is two characters that represent a special character. Notes converts the compose sequence into the correct symbol. For more help, see "Special Characters" on page 82.

Cursor

The cursor is the active spot on your screen. It can take many forms: an arrow, a flashing vertical line, an hourglass, a two-headed arrow, etc.

Cursor (Example)

Cursor Keys

The cursor keys are the keys that control the position of the *cursor*. They include the directional arrow keys (<←>, <→>, <↑>, and <↓>), <Home>, <End>, <Page Up>, and <Page Down>.

Database

A Notes database is a collection of *documents*, all of which share certain pre-defined characteristics. These characteristics can be minimal or complex.

Database Window

A database window displays a *database's* current *view*. A database has only one database window open at a time.

Dialog Box

A dialog box is a collection of controls and features that you use to perform tasks or set properties. A dialog box has a title bar at its top and a border around its contents.

Document

In Notes, information resides in documents, and documents reside in *databases*. A Notes document can contain many different types of data. The typical Notes document is all or mostly text, but a document can also contain graphics, embedded files from other software packages, even multimedia elements.

Document Window

A document window is a *secondary window* that displays a *document*.

Double-Click

Double-clicking is just like *clicking* only you press the *primary mouse button* twice in rapid succession. If you can't get the hang of double-clicking, your mouse's double-click speed may be set too fast. Ask your technical support person or a knowledgeable friend or coworker for help.

Dragging-and-Dropping

A technique for moving items with the mouse. You point at the item with the *cursor*, press the *primary mouse button* to "grab" the item, "drag" it by moving the mouse, and "drop" it by releasing the mouse button.

Drop Down Box

Drop down boxes appear in *dialog boxes*. You use a drop down box to set a property or select an option. A closed drop down box is a narrow horizontal rectangle with a down arrow *button* at the right end. You open a drop down box by *clicking* on its down arrow button.

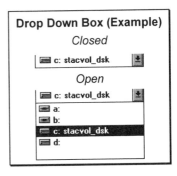

Edit Mode

To edit a *document* you must put it in edit mode, which means that you can edit the contents of some or all of the document's *fields*. When a document is in edit mode, you can see brackets at the beginning and end of each *editable field*.

Editable Field

An editable field is exactly that, a *field* that you can edit.

Field

A field is the space in a document that is set aside for a certain piece of information. A simple document might consist of a field for the title, a field for the author, and a field for the document's body.

Font

Notes uses "font" to mean both a typeface alone <u>and</u> the entire set of formatting properties applied to a given piece of text. In this book, "font" always means the entire set of formatting properties.

Form

A form is a template that contains the necessary *fields* for a certain type of *document*. You use a form as the basis for a new document.

Group Box

Group boxes appear in *dialog boxes*. A group box is a labeled rectangle that contains a related group of controls and features.

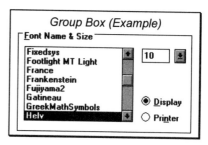

Groupware

Groupware is software that allows groups of users to work together by sharing information across a computer network.

Hot Keys

Hot keys are a simultaneous combination of keys that accesses a feature or function. Synonyms: *accelerator keys, short-cut keys.*

Icon

An icon is a small picture that represents a program, a function, a data file, or anything that a programmer wants it to. The most common use of icons is to represent programs that can be launched from the Windows Shell. For most users, the Windows Shell is Program Manager.

Index

An index is a separate file that Notes uses to process full text queries. For more help, see "Searching a Database" on page 133.

Insertion Point

When you're editing text, the insertion point is where Notes will insert new text. It is either the *cursor* or the currently highlighted text. Notes will delete highlighted text when you start typing.

List Box

List boxes appear in *dialog boxes*. You use a list box to select one item from a list of like items. You select an item by *clicking* on it, or by using the *cursor keys* to highlight it.

List Box (Example)

Main Window

A program's main window encompasses and controls the important functional areas that you use to do your work.

Maximized

A *window* is maximized when it occupies all of its available space.

On/Off Property

Rich text fields accept ten *font* properties. The on/off properties — normal, bold, italic, strikethrough, superscript, and subscript — have only two settings, on and off. Turning the Normal Property on deactivates the other six on/off properties.

Plain Text Field

All you can do in a plain text field is add and remove characters. When you're in a plain text field, the typeface indicator and point size indicator on the Status Bar (see page 13) are blank.

Primary Mouse Button

On a two-button mouse, the primary button is the one that you use more often. For most users, it's the left button. If you're left-handed, your buttons may be reversed, in which case the primary button would be on the right.

Replica / Replication

Replication maintains copies, called replicas, of a shared *database*. The changes that users make to each replica are periodically transmitted to the shared database and to the other replicas. For more help, see "What Is Replication?" on page 159.

Required Fields

A required field is a *field* which must be filled in before you can save the *document*.

Response Document

A *document* that is affiliated with another document is called a *response document*.

Rich Text Field

Rich text fields accept text formatting, paragraph formatting, special characters, tables, OLE objects, and Notes special document features (doclinks, pop-ups, buttons, and attachments).

Scroll Bar

Scroll bars come in two versions, horizontal and vertical. You use them to view text or graphics that won't fit in a

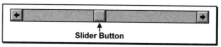
Slider Button

window, or in some cases, to adjust values. You use a scroll bar by moving the slider button. Point at the slider button with the mouse, press the *primary mouse button*, and drag it in the direction you want to go. You can also move the slider button by *clicking* on either side of it, or by clicking on the arrow buttons at either end of the scroll bar.

Secondary Mouse Button

On a two-button mouse, the secondary button is the one that you use less often. For most users, it's the right button. If you're left-handed, your buttons may be reversed, in which case the secondary button would be on the left.

Secondary Window

In general, a secondary window is where you get your hands on the data. In a word processor, the secondary windows are where you edit the text of the open files. In Notes, the secondary windows are where you work with *databases* and *documents*.

Server

In Notes, a server is a computer that houses *databases*. A server can be your own PC, or a computer on your network that serves as a database library.

Short-Cut Keys

Short-cut keys are a simultaneous combination of keys that accesses a feature or function. Synonyms: *accelerator keys, hot keys*.

Sub-Menu

A sub-menu opens out next to the parent menu selection. Menu selections that open a sub-menu are followed by a small wedge ("▶").

Text Box

Text boxes appear in *dialog boxes*. You use a text box to specify text for a given task, such as naming a file. You access a text box by *clicking* in it, by pressing <Tab> until the

Text Box and Label (Example)
Filename:

text box receives input, or if the text has a label with an underlined letter, by pressing <Alt> plus the letter. You enter text by typing it in.

Variable Property

Rich text fields accept ten *font* properties. The variable properties — typeface, point size, and color — have a range of settings. For example, Notes offers fifteen different text colors.

View

A view is a full or partial list of a *database's documents*. Views appear in *database windows*.

Window

A window is a rectangular area where you do a certain type of work. A window has a title bar at its top and a border around its contents. In Notes, there are four types of windows: the *Main Window*, the *Workspace Window*, *database windows*, and *document windows*

Workspace / Workspace Window

The documentation that comes with Notes refers to the *Main Window* as the "Workspace", but Notes also has an important *secondary window* with the same name. In this book, "Workspace" always refers to the secondary window.

Index

About Database dialog box, 20
Above property, 109
Accented letters, 86-89
Accent Sensitive search option, 50, 134
Accept button, 65
Access Control List, 17, 34
Access Level Indicator, 16
Active window, 8n
Adding icons, 26-27
Address Book drop down box, 151
Address Book icon, 152
Address books, 152-154
Address Book window, 151-154
Align Center command, 110
Align Full command, 110
Align Left command, 110
Alignment drop down box, 108
Alignment property, 105, 108
Align None command, 110
Align Right command, 110
All Checked button, 127
All Databases in Common option, 162
All of These Words drop down box, 141
All option button, 129
ANSI character set, 82
Append command, 62
Apply button, 114
Arithmetic symbols, 83

Attachments, 44-47, 67-70
Available Icons list box, 170

Backwards search option, 50, 135
Below property, 109
Bold property, 99, 100, 103
Borders Visible option, 80
Buttons, 44, 47, 70

Calling servers, 158
Call Server dialog box, 158
Cancel button, 127
Cascade selection, 173
Case Sensitive Index option, 136
Case Sensitive search option, 50, 134
Categorize dialog box, 124, 125
Categorizing documents, 124-125
Cell borders, 90, 97
Cell Borders group box, 97
Clear command, 62
Clicking, 5n
Close command, 175
Closing
    active documents, 53
    databases, 25
    secondary windows, 177
Collapse All command, 40, 42
Collapse command, 40, 42
Color display box, 102

Color property, 99-101
Column Bar, 24
Columns, table
    adding, 91-92
    deleting, 92-93
    formatting, 95-96
Combo box, 19*n*
Command Priority, 41
Compose sequences, 82-89
Compress option, 70
Contracting views, 40-42
Control box, 8
Control menu, 8
Copies text box, 128
Copy command, 62, 126
Copying documents, 126
Copy option, 108, 160
Correct button, 65
Created option, 121
Creating
    databases, 29-33
    documents, 56-59
    full text indices, 135-137
    new set of SmartIcons, 171
    OLE objects, 74-78
    paragraph styles, 114-115
    tables, 89-93
Currency symbols, 83
Current Set list box, 170
Custom Forms, 150
Customizing SmartIcons, 169-172
Cut command, 62, 126
Cutting and pasting, 62, 126

Database icons, 11, 12
    managing, 25-29
    opening databases from, 22-23
Database Information dialog box,
    22
Database list box, 19

Databases
    conventional, 3-4
    defined, 4
    Help, 179
    mail, *see* Mail
    searching, *see* Searching
        databases
    working with, 17-34
        Access Control Lists, 34
        closing, 25
        creating, 29-33
        database windows, 23-25
        deleting, 33
        managing database icons, 25-
        29
        opening, 17-23
Database views, *see* Views
Database windows, 23-25
Date
    full text searches and, 142
    selecting documents by, 120-
        121
    setting, 167-168
Daylight Savings Time, 167
Define button, 65
Delete button, 117
Delete Index, 139
Delete Row/Column dialog box,
    92
Deleting
    databases, 33
    document categories, 125
    documents, 126-127
    full text indices, 139
    paragraph styles, 116-117
    rows and columns in tables, 92-
        93
    sets of SmartIcons, 172
    tables, 93
Deselect All, 61
Detach button, 45, 47

Directories list box, 47, 69, 73
Discussion Template, 30
Disk drives, selecting, 68
Display Area, 24
Doclinks, 44, 47-48, 70-71
Document Library Template, 30
Document options (documents
      only), 129-130
Documents
  defined, 4
  forwarding, 153-155
  See also Editing: documents;
      Managing documents;
      Reading documents;
      Views
Document Separation drop down
      box, 130
Document Separation option, 130
Document windows, 43
Done button, 65, 115, 117
Double-clicking
  Notes icon and, 5
  title bar and, 8
Draft Quality option, 52, 129
Dragging-and-dropping, 28, 112
Drive drop down box, 68

Editable field, 58, 59
Edit Clear command, 29
Edit Find Next command, 50
Editing
  documents, 55-66
    creating, 56-59
    cutting and pasting, 62
    edit mode, 58, 59
    Edit Undo command, 62
    fields, 55-56
    headers and footers, 63-64
    insertion point positioning,
      60-66

saving changes, 65-66
selecting text with keyboard,
    61
selecting text with mouse, 61
SmartIcons for, 56
spelling checks, 64-65
paragraph styles, 115-116
rich text, 67-97
  attachments, 67-70
  buttons, 70
  doclinks, 70-71
  importing files, 72-74
  OLE objects, 74-78
  pop-ups, 79-81
  resizing pictures, 81-82
  special characters, 82-89
  tables, *see* Tables
sets of SmartIcons, 170
workspace tabs, 12-13
Editing option, 108
Editing symbols, 83
Edit mode, 58, 59
Edit Table Format dialog box, 94,
    95
Edit Undo command, 62
Enlarge Point Size command,
    102, 103
Enter Password Dialog Box, 5, 6,
    165
Exchange Document Read Marks
    option, 163
Exclude Documents with These
    Words text box, 142
Exiting, 6
Expand All command, 40, 42
Expand command, 40, 42
Expanding views, 40-42

Field help, 55
Fields, 55-56, 66

File Attachment Information
 dialog box, 45
File Full Text Search sub-menu,
 138, 145
File Name combo box, 32, 69, 73
File Name text box, 32
File Print dialog box, 51-52, 128
Find All button, 135
Find and Replace dialog box, 49
Find dialog box, 133-134
Find Documents Stored drop
 down box, 142
Find Next button, 50, 135
Fit to Window option, 90, 95
Floating help windows, 178
Font dialog box, 100-102
Font Name list box, 101
Font properties, 99-100
Fonts, applying, 99-104
Footers, 63-64
Formatting
 rich text, 99-117
  applying fonts, 99-104
  paragraph properties, 105-
   112
  paragraph styles, 112-117
 tables, 94-97
Form Override option, 130
Forms, 57
Forwarding documents, 153-155
Fraction symbols, 84
Full Text Create Index dialog box,
 136
Full text indices, 135-140
Full Text Information dialog box,
 138
Full text search, 140-145

Geometry symbols, 83
Global settings, 94-95

Groupware, 2-3
Guess button, 65

Hang Up button, 159
Hang Up dialog box, 159
Hang Up When Done option, 163
Headers, 63-64
Help, 10, 55, 177-180
Help database, 179
Help menu, 179
Help windows, 178
Hide group box, 108
Hide options, 105, 108

Icons
 database, *see* Database icons
 defined, 5*n*
 Notes, 5
 SmartIcons (tool bar), *see*
  SmartIcons (tool bar)
Icon Size button, 170
Ignore button, 65
Import dialog box, 72
Importing files, 72-74
Include Word Variants option,
 143
Indent command, 110
Indent First Line command, 110
Indents, 110, 112
Index Breaks option, 137
Indexing databases, 135-137
Indices, full text, 135-140
Inherit Future Design Changes
 Option, 32
Insert Attachments dialog box,
 68
Insertion point
 defined, 14*n*
 positioning of, 60-66

Insert Object Choose File dialog box, 76-77
Insert Object dialog box, 75
Insert Object Display Format dialog box, 75
Insert PopUp dialog box, 79-80
Insert Row/Column dialog box, 91
Insert Table dialog box, 89-90
Interline property, 109
Italic property, 99, 100, 103

Jump From document, 71
Jump To document, 70
Justification (text alignment), 96

Keep Lines Together option, 107
Keep with Next Paragraph option, 107
Keyboard
    instructions, 1-2
    manipulating secondary windows with, 175-177
    selecting text with, 61

Launch button, 45
Left margin, table, 95
Limits, common, 181
List Files of Type drop down box, 73
Location Setup dialog box, 167
Logging on to a network, 5-6
Lotus Multibyte Character Set (LMBCS), 82-89
Lotus Notes
    benefits of, 3
    vs. conventional database programs, 3-4

defined, 2-3
exiting, 6
logging on to a network, 5-6
starting, 5
use of, 4-5

Mail, 4, 147-155, 161
    address books, 152-153
    forwarding documents, 153-155
    opening, 149-150
    SmartIcons, 147
    as specialized, enhanced set of databases, 147
    using over a modem, 148-149, 152, 155
    writing, 150-152
Mail.Box database, 149
Mail Compose sub-menu, 150
Mail File text box, 149
Mail forms, 150
Mail Indicator, 15
Mail Setup dialog box, 148
Mail Type Indicator, 16
Main documents, 36
Main window, 7-16
    menu bar, 9-10
    SmartIcons (tool bar), 10-11
    status bar, 13-16
    title bar, 8-9
    Workspace Window, 7, 11-13
Managing documents, 119-131
    categorizing, 124-125
    copying, 126
    deleting, 126-127
    marking read and unread, 122-123
    moving, 126
    printing, 128-131
    selecting, 119-121

Margins
    paragraph, 105-107, 111-112
    table, 95
Margins group box, 106
Marker Bar, 24-25
Markers, inserting, 63
Maximize All selection, 173
Maximize button, 9, 174
Maximize command, 175
Maximized window, 8*n*
Maximum Number of Results
        option, 143
Menu bar, 9-10
Menu selections, 9
    descriptions of, 10
    for formatting paragraphs, 109,
        110
    help for, 10, 55
    secondary windows, 173
    view, 40-42
Message Area, 14
Minimize All selection, 173
Minimize button, 9, 174
Minimize command, 175
Modems, 157-163
    calling a server, 158
    hanging up, 159
    remote SmartIcons, 157
    replication, 159-163
        creating replicas, 160-161
        defined, 159
        performing, 161-163
    set up, 157
    using mail over, 148-149, 152,
        155
Modifications, 165-172
    date and time settings, 167-
        168
    password changing, 165-166
    printer selection, 168
Modified option, 121

Mouse
    manipulating windows with,
        174
    selecting text with, 61
Move command, 175, 176
Moving documents, 126
Moving icons, 28

Network Activity Indicator, 14
Networks, logging on to, 5-6
New button, 115, 161
New Categories text box, 124, 125
New Database dialog box, 30-31
New Database settings, 32
New Replica dialog box, 160-161
New Style Name text box, 114
Next command, 175
Non-English letters, 84
Normal property, 99, 100, 103
Notes documents, *see* Documents
Notes Help, 177-180
Notes Mail, *see* Mail

Object Type list box, 75
OK button, 52, 78, 80, 121, 131,
        137, 149, 163
OLE (Object Linking and
        Embedding), 74-78
One or More of These Words text
        box, 142
Only Current button, 127
On/Off commands, 41
On/Off properties, 99, 102, 103
Open Database dialog box, 18,
        26
Opening
    attachments, 45
    databases, 17-23
    documents, 43

mail, 149-150
menus, 9
Operating systems, 1

Page Break Before Paragraph
    option, 107
Page Break command, 110
Page Range group box, 52,
    129
Pages, 11, 12
Pagination options, 105, 107
Paging through databases, 51
Paragraph properties, 105-112
Paragraph styles, 112-117
Password
    changing, 165-166
    entering, 5
Paste command, 62, 126
Personal address books, 153
Pictures, resizing, 81-82
Plain text fields, 56
Plain text search, 133-135
Point Size Indicator, 15, 104
Point size property, 99-101
Pop-ups, 44, 48, 79-81
Positioning buttons, 9
Printer selection, 168
Printing
    active documents, 51-52
    views and documents, 128-131
Printing option, 108
Print Selected Documents, 129
Print Setup dialog box, 168
Print View, 129
Program Manager, 5
Punctuation symbols, 85

Query Builder dialog box, 140-
    142

Reading documents, 43-53
    attachments, 44-47
    buttons, 44, 47
    closing active document, 53
    doclinks, 44, 47-48
    navigating, 44
    opening, 43
    paging through databases, 51
    pop-ups, 44, 48
    printing active document, 51-
        52
    searching for text, 49-50
Reading option, 108
Read marks, 122-123
Receive Documents from Server
    option, 163
Reduce Point Size command, 102,
    103
Refreshing views, 42, 127
Refresh Panel, 25
Remote use, *see* Modems
Removing icons, 29
Replicate Database Templates
    option, 163
Replicate options, 162-163
Replication, 159-163
    creating replicas, 160-161
    defined, 159
    performing, 161-163
Required fields, 58-59, 66
Reset Page Numbers option, 130
Resizing pictures, 81-82
Response documents, 37
Restore button, 9, 174
Restore command, 175
Rich text fields
    defined, 56
    See also Editing: rich text;
        Formatting: rich text
Rows, table
    adding, 91-92

deleting, 92-93
formatting, 95-96
Ruler, 111-112
Run in Background option,
    163

Save Set button, 171
Saving
    attachments, 45, 46
    changes, 65-66, 169
    documents, 58
Scroll bar, 20n
Search bar, 144-145
Search button, 144, 145
Searching databases, 133-145
    full text indices, 135-140
    full text search, 140-145
    plain text search, 133-135
Searching for text, 49-50
Search options, 50, 142-143
Search Options dialog box, 142-
    143
Search Selected Documents, 134
Search Within View, 134
Secondary mouse button, 10n
Secondary windows
    database, 23-25
    defined, 7n
    document, 43
    manipulating, 173-177
    Workspace, 7, 11-13
Select All, 61
Select by Date dialog box, 120-121
Selected Database(s) option, 162
Selected in View option, 143
Send Documents to Server
    option, 163
Servers, 17, 19, 21, 27, 31, 32, 158
Set drop down box, 170, 171
Set Password dialog box, 165-166

Show Only Categories command,
    40, 42
Show Only Search Results
    command, 40-42
Show Only Selected command,
    40-42
Show Only Unread command,
    40, 42, 122
Show Page Breaks option, 106
Show Results options, 143-144
Show Ruler command, 110
Show Search Bar, 145
Size command, 175
SmartIcons dialog box, 169
SmartIcons (tool bar), 10-11
    customizing, 169-172
    for editing documents, 56
    for formatting paragraphs, 110
    for formatting text, 103
    mail, 147
    for paging through databases,
        51
    Read/Unread, 123
    remote, 157
    for views, 38, 39
SmartIcons button, 15
Sorted by Date (Ascending)
    option, 143
Sorted by Date (Descending)
    option, 143
Sorted by Relevance option, 143
Spacing properties, 105, 109
Special characters, 82-89
Spelling checks, 64-65
Status bar, 13-16, 104
Stopping Notes, 177
Stop Word File option, 136-137
Strikethrough property, 99, 100
Style Name list box, 114, 117
Subdirectories, 19, 27, 73
Sub-menus, 21, 22

Subscript property, 99, 100
Superscript property, 99, 100

Tables, 89-97
    adding rows and columns, 91-92
    creating, 89-90
    deleting, 93
    deleting rows and columns in, 92-93
    formatting, 94-97
Tabs, 105, 107, 111, 112
Tab stops, 64
Templates, creating new databases with, 29-33
Template Servers dialog box, 31
Text alignment, 96
Text fields
    defined, 56
    rich, *see* Editing: rich text;
        Formatting: rich text
Text menu, 102, 103
Text Paragraph dialog box, 105-109
Text Paragraph Styles dialog box, 112-114
Things to Do Template, 30
Tile selection, 173
Time setting, 167-168
Title bar, 8-9
Tool bar, *see* SmartIcons
Tools Check Spelling dialog box, 64-65
Tools Replicate dialog box, 162
Tools Unread Marks sub-menu, 122-123

Transfer Outgoing Mail option, 163
Typeface Indicator, 14, 104
Typeface property, 99-101

Underline property, 99, 100, 103
Undo Delete, 127
Unread mail, scanning, 150
Unread marks, 122-123
Update Index, 139

Variable properties, 99
Views, 35-42
    categories and documents, 36-37
    defined, 23
    expanding and contracting, 40-42
    function of, 35
    navigating, 38-39
    opening to, 23
    printing, 128-131
    refreshing, 42, 127
    selecting, 38
    SmartIcons for, 38, 39

Whole Word search option, 50, 134
Windows, *see* Main window;
    Secondary windows
Windows Shell, 5*n*
Workspace Page Name dialog box, 13
Workspace Window, 7, 11-13
Writing mail, 150-152

ABOUT THE AUTHOR

ALLEN SIM is a self-employed writer of software manuals who lives and works in the fine borough of Brooklyn. He was born in Michigan, spent most of his youth in Pennsylvania, and moved to New York City to complete his education and find a career.

In 1987, Mr. Sim graduated magna cum laude from New York University with a degree in economics. Displaying vast originality, boldness, and depth of imagination, he took a job on Wall Street. After four years in finance (which is pronounced like "finesse" by people from the right families), Mr. Sim quit his job to write fiction. Luckily, he took with him a certain facility with computers, which, by a crooked path too tiresome to mention, led to his current occupation, and hence this book.

Mr. Sim is very happily married and is the father of a toddler son. He sporadically works on an unfinished novel and an unfinished screenplay. There are at least three more novels and a similar number of other screenplays rattling around in his head. If this book sells well, he may find time to finish the first two, and that would be a great relief to him. (Not that he's hinting.)